Federico Capeci

Post Millennial Marketing
The biggest change in marketing ever led by New Generations.
If we allow them to drive it.

*For my "centennial" Alice
and my Ludovico,
whose generation doesn't yet have a name.*

CONTENTS

Preface by Dario Gargiulio, Global Chief Marketing Officer, Diesel

Introduction
    Marketing as a snapshot of society
    Marketing doesn't work like it used to
    From Generation 2.0 to Millennials
    Data sources and methodology

Chapter 1 – What hasn't changed since we began
    Segments, needs, expectations: the starting point of marketing
    From audience to target markets: mass marketing vs personalisation
    From consumer to prosumer: sales vs co-creation
    From client to stakeholder: customer centricity
    Generations as segments in marketing

Chapter 2 – What we have experienced
    Baby Boomer Marketing: needs, values and expectations
    Generation X Marketing: needs, values and expectations

Chapter 3 – Where we are now: the Millennial Bang
    Who Millennials are
    The post-Millennials, or Centennials
    Millennials and Centennials in figures
    Millennials and the digital world
    Millennials and myths to be dismantled (with statistics)

Chapter 4 – The S.T.Y.L.E. of Millennials
    Millennial-consumers: needs and values (S.T.Y.L.E.)
- Sociability
- Transparency
- Yes, now!
- Liberty
- Experience

    How many Millennials

Chapter 5 – The Future: Post Millennial Marketing

"Millennialism" is not just about following a new target market
How marketing will change (the implications of S.T.Y.L.E.)
The Post Millennial Marketing framework:
- Listen to Markets: actively listening to consumers
- Pop-up in Moments: appearing at specific, relevant times
- Surprise with Contents: being strange, unexpected and provocative
- Facilitate Action: laying out and facilitating the action that you expect
- Enrich Experience: enriching touch points with experience
- Connect with Brand Purpose: connecting with the brand and the role that it has for the consumer

The Millennial @Work: expectations and realities of Millennials in a company environment

Conclusions

Afterword by Marialuisa Pezzali, author and presenter at Radio 24, Il Sole 24 Ore Group

Bibliography

PREFACE

I didn't like this book. Or perhaps it would be more accurate to say that I don't like to face up to the truths it piles up in a simple but unavoidable way.

Everyone who loves marketing knows that one of the main problems is recognising change. In part because society evolves much faster than corporate communication models or those who want to communicate a message, and mainly because – after so much effort expended in trying to understand the target market – you realise that you have to reconsider everything and start learning from scratch.

But it is precisely that consideration which underlies the pages that lie ahead of you. There are those who talk about Baby Boomers, Millennials or Centennials, but Federico Capeci makes us realise that we should stop running after hordes of consumers in the hope of encasing them in a definition. The author shifts attention to a change in values, politely discounting age ranges or sterile terms that provided a rational framework for market research, but did so without telling us anything about the underlying movements of the users, the consumers, or simply people who have no desire to be straitjacketed by labels or definitions.

Federico's intuition has been to talk of "New Generation Marketing" by starting from what happened yesterday. Ably bringing together a critical point of view on the evolution of target markets over the past few decades with an impeccable analysis on the inadequateness of those who are again seeking to offer communication models to generations who nowadays have neither the time nor the inclination to listen to messages that fall from above.

The keystone of the themes dealt with in this book is, I believe, awareness, a term that is often misused in discussions about marketing.

Over the next few years a lot of books and essays will be published telling us the story of this historic moment, but only a few people are able to make that analysis right now, as the change is taking place.

It is probably the first time since the industrial revolution that we find ourselves faced by such a disruptive social turning point. The comparison is a reflection of the speed with which this change has occurred and is materialising. If we just look at Ikea or Ryanair, without even touching upon Facebook and Amazon, we can state that an unstoppable process of democratisation is taking place, towards a market that most of the time is exposed by consumers themselves as they fight back against the asymmetric nature of information which, until a few years ago, lay behind the fortune of brands.

In this situation we find ourselves faced by three generations which are completely different from one another. In the middle are those who, like me, have a harder time, or those who both experienced a phone box and Facetime. But Millennials, by contrast, aren't concerned with categorising or observing what is taking place right behind them and they are probably also less interested in understanding which social phenomenon they belong to, given that probably one of the few certainties that they have is that the world around them will change even faster.

I was talking about this very issue when Federico and I met for the first time. We were discussing qualitative research when I was just setting out, and I perfectly remember my diffidence over the analysis of random target markets on the creative projects that I was developing. Already then his ability lay in not addressing a marketing plan by decoding the target market, in not making a value judgement based on the words of those he had listened to, but to offer some reflections on the relevance of the message. Nowadays we all talk about data and controlling information, the miraculous answers to all the problems of those who are trying to establish a media or communication strategy; but now, as then, Federico has taught me to look at a piece of data as the confirmation of a "good intention" or as the quantification of a risk. (Whether that risk is taken or not will then determine the kind of manager that will hold one role or another).

At a very different stage of my career, when there was still widespread scepticism amongst the brands – even the most advanced ones – over whether to join in a conversation, to step down to meet consumers as equals and no longer look down from on high, Federico and I discussed the Facebook phenomenon. He saw me as the right interlocutor to offer interesting ideas on what position to take on this strange animal that in just a few weeks was overtaking giants like MySpace or Yahoo! in terms of traffic. It seems like a good time to apologise, seeing that I didn't understand a thing! For years I fell into the trap of building up fanbases, being taken in by the mirage of organic conversations with fans and the "likes" that followed. Until the point when, belatedly – but nevertheless before a lot of others – I realised that brands and marketing teams were simply puppets managed by the particular algorithm that was working at that time.

If today we talk about Post Millennial Marketing, there are only a few fixed points, but the sooner these are taken on board, the sooner we can navigate these changes with credibility.

Now is the time to put down our arms and stop hunting target markets. For too long the obsession of recruiting young consumers has distracted marketers from having to worry about creating relevant content which is worthy of being commented on or shared.

In this complex, uneven and schizophrenic situation, in which audiences are running away from traditional media, people are disaffected by information policies and organisations. It is precisely the love brands that have the unique opportunity to be able to inspire and touch in an authentic way the mind and the heart of this elusive generation.

Dario Gargiulo
Global Chief Marketing Officer, Diesel

INTRODUCTION

Marketing as a snapshot of society

Each generation gets the marketing that it deserves.

How ridiculous those 1980s television adverts look, with the kids of the time with their hair bouffant with hairspray, with puffed up shoulders under coloured jackets, with American jeans belted high and the all-important turn-ups at the bottom...: advertising with people who were always happy, smiling, singing songs with perfect rhymes, carefully tuneful, with lively colourful writing over the screen.

That is how marketing saw us.

Some of the advertising from the past really makes us smile when we find it on YouTube or see it posted by people of our own age on Facebook! If you were to close your eyes and try to remember one of these adverts for a moment, I am sure that, from outside, I would see your eyes soften.

Perhaps it is tough to admit it, but those adverts talked to us, they really talked about us, exactly as we were at that time. So in some way we find them touching, because they remind us of what we were like, they bring back some of the times from our youth.

I get the same feeling when I see my mother flicking through the magazines that are stacked in the attic. The ones that, I don't know how, reappear regularly every Christmas, from the boxes close to those with the decorations. She flicks through the magazine, reads the headlines and doesn't dwell on the text: nowadays the content would be boring to read, but she stops and looks at the adverts, looks again, and calls me to tell me that this or that product that she really liked isn't made any more, or to tell me of her satisfaction, which is practically gratitude, that she still has this other brand in the kitchen. The tone used in the adverts also makes her smile, but they bring out the same positive, recognition emotions which advertising from thirty years ago brings out in me: advertising from our youth is like a motorway that we can use to swiftly reconnect with the memories and with that part of ourselves which is not much considered in daily life. That is what happens when marketing works: it talks to us, and about us, both at the time and years later.

My grandmother is no longer with us, but I am sure that she would experience a visit to the Museum of the Twentieth Century in Milan in a much more intense way: what for me are works of art, for her would be the advertising posters which she had seen at a precise moment in her life, like open books of memories which are reconnected to the present through a slogan, a product, or a brand. A poster is a whole bar, it is the music from the 75rpm records of the time, it is her when she was young.

The adverts from the twentieth century talk about a time when my grandmother was young, the ones from the 1960s talk about when my mother was young, the 1980s television ads remind me of when I myself was young... and what about today's advertising? To whom, and about whom is it talking?

To understand if, and to what extent, marketing now is talking to young people, we should ask Millennials, today's generation of young people. Unfortunately we have the answer: only 19% of Millennials say they see themselves in today's advertising[1]. What is happening? What is marketing talking about, and to whom?

Marketing doesn't work like it used to

Marketing has always known how to talk to young people, but nowadays it doesn't work any more, because it has been conceived for Generation X, and not for Millennials. The problem is that young people today are very different from those in the past, and "post-Millennial" society can't be seen and managed with continuity approaches derived from what doesn't exist any more; a new mentality is needed.

Even though there are undoubtedly huge differences between Baby Boomer Marketing and the subsequent Generation X Marketing, there is also some continuity: the economic and demographic boom which marketing directors of those times operated in gave the marketing directors of the next generation the great masses to manage and to convert to consumption. A kind of marketing is the logical evolution of the other; one has received the baton and the history of its predecessor.

By contrast, Post Millennial Marketing, whose beginning we are seeing, is bound to be dramatically different, and truly new, because from a certain

---

[1] Research on "Donne di domani" *(Women of Tomorrow)* (https://goo.gl/j1XyBo) conducted by Kantar TNS for Danone in March 2015, sample of 1,000 women aged 15-25 (CAWI interviews)

time onwards it is society itself, led by young people, which has radically changed in its essence, in how it communicates, in how relationships and values – both cultural and economic – are created. It is different in how it uses media, it is different in its tastes in advertising and it is different in its consumption.

So marketing aimed at Baby Boomers (those born between 1945 and 1964) was marketing that talked of positivity and the future, and the marketing for Generation X (those born between the 1970s and before the 1990s) was marketing in response to the society of conformity and consumption of those years. But marketing for Generations Y and Z (those born after the mid-1980s, who are also called Millennials and Centennials) is, should or will be, marketing for the connected society, which is being created with the youth of today.

Unfortunately, not many companies today are correctly interpreting the contemporary world, and often when they talk about young people they put forward stereotypes or, still worse, they talk about – and to – a world that has gone, particularly that of Generation X. Unfortunately, there is an abyss between the need to conform felt by the youth of the 80s, and the desire to be connected felt by young people today: marketing aimed at the first group aggregates and makes uniform, whereas connected marketing starts from single identities and respects individual expression, around a shared sense of relationships and group meaning. Generation X marketing is made up of advertisements and television commercials; Millennials marketing is composed of *storytelling* and is digital. 1980s marketing is top-down; post-2000 marketing is participatory and "convocative". Unfortunately, a lot of marketing directors who should understand and communicate with Millennials, are themselves part of Generation X and perhaps as a consequence misunderstand a generation which is so different from their own.

It is in this abyss between old and new marketing – so marketing created after the Millennial (Big) Bang – that today's marketing directors are losing themselves as they struggle with communication methods which are no longer effective, and the uncertainty over good practice in the world that is emerging.

This book seeks to reduce this gap, providing logical frameworks that bring together the past and the present, to then take the path to

Post Millennial Marketing, thanks to the recognition and assessment of the differences in the current context from that of yesterday.

We will thus start from the marketing of the past, so as to appreciate a world that no longer exists and the reasons for the current ineffectiveness. This is also to identify what hasn't actually changed and what will not change as long as we can talk of marketing: the biggest risk in economic disciplines is losing historical memory and thus no longer being able to distinguish what really is new from what, by contrast, is just an updating of valid concepts from the past.

In Chapter I we will look at the various ways in which marketing segments its consumers, and put forward the newest approaches together with the most-established ones, many aspects of which are now being questioned.

In Chapter II, we will go right into the heart of marketing for generations, using landmark cases in our description of Baby Boomer Marketing, and then Generation X Marketing.

Finally, in Chapter III, we will deal head on with the change taking place in society, describing Millennials and Centennials: they are the new generation of young people, the consumers who are leading the change and who lay down the rules of the new marketing, "Post Millennial Marketing". After them (and because of them) nothing can, and nothing should, stay the same as before.

From Generation 2.0 to Millennials

In this book we will make several references to a previous work "Generazione 2.0. Chi sono, cosa vogliono, come dialogare con loro." *(Generation 2.0. Who they are, what they want and how to talk to them.* Federico Capeci, 2014, published by. Franco Angeli): a text that had the privilege of taking the debate on this generation – which too often is misunderstood, misinterpreted, stereotyped and mistreated – into academic and professional areas, and on various mass media right up to the Italian Parliament (http://goo.gl/rp9RgU). The reference framework on Millennials provided by the book (in the text, the young people in question were actually called "Generation 2.0", since the term "Millennials" wasn't yet in common usage, in the way it is now) is very deep and up to date, thanks to extensive study work conducted over the years, which has supplied the theoretical basis: so in the current text we will take up a lot of the concepts used then, but we will take a deeper look at the awareness of young people from a marketing perspective, and specify details and segments in an international context. The data and considerations on Millennials will also be updated with more recent studies and research, and – together with this – we will look deeper at our knowledge of Generation Z, the so-called Centennials, who were born after the 2000s.

Once the target market – and thus the true driver of the change taking place – has been described, in Chapter IV we will illustrate the implications for contemporary marketing, using the same S.T.Y.L.E. key to interpreting, put forward in "#Generation 2.0". Post Millennial Marketing has a defined S.T.Y.L.E. (sociability, transparency, "yes and now", liberty, experience): it invents and suggests marketing initiatives that should be social and shareable, transparent and real, immediate and reactive, free and experiential. Concrete cases and referrals will also help us to clarify the most theoretical concepts to set out on a course of change.

But you shouldn't expect real conclusions: if at the end you like this book, it will be because it has posed questions on what people have told you so far about marketing, without giving recipes or prescriptive lists (which, amongst other things, would end up growing year by year, like Kotler's "P"s[2]). Post Millennial Marketing puts itself forward as supplying

---

[2] This is a reference to Philip Kotler's "four P" marketing mix model, which states that operational marketing activity can be handled through four "P"s:

elements and logical frameworks to formulate answers to questions which are still open amongst a lot of marketing professionals, and its ambition is to equip readers with the fundamental ingredients to try out, experiment and themselves create their own marketing recipe, following the S.T.Y.L.E. of Millennials.

Data sources and methodology

This text draws on numerous studies on Millennials and on digital marketing, many of which have been personally led by the author over the years.

For most recent data and an international perspective, extensive use has been made of various studies carried out by Kantar (www.kantar.com) at both an Italian and global level, such as – but not only - "Connected Life" (http://connectedlife.tnsglobal.com) by Kantar TNS and "AdReaction" by Kantar Millward Brown (www.millwardbrown.com/adreaction/genxyz).

Every marketing concept present in this book, just as in the previous "#Generation 2.0" work, thus comes from data, facts, words and thoughts from real people who have been interviewed and not just from desktop theorising: a new perspective on marketing can only start from the observations from consumers, and from the new, emerging dynamics, which are well represented by Millennials, who are so different from previous generations.

Product, Price, Placement and Promotion. Over time various elements have been put forward to integrate into the model, with the addition of Packaging, Personal selling, service (the product-service concept) and others, so we thus end up looking at five Ps, six Ps and so on.

Chapter I – WHAT HASN'T CHANGED SINCE WE BEGAN

Segments and needs: the starting point of marketing

There is just one organisation in the world that can do without marketing (at least in the way we understand it in this book) and can address all its interlocutors in the same way: the **Church**. It has a great product with a fantastic promise: eternal salvation; a formidable price strategy, following the most modern rules on *freemium*[3]: free access to base services and offers which change according to what the client wants to pay, or services used on special occasions; very wide distribution: a church tower in every corner of the world, well positioned in the city centre in a way that not even the best banks manage to do; a cutting-edge communication strategy, based on a successful opinion leader, on social approval and impressive word of mouth. Marketing's 4 Ps have been used in the best possible way, and that has actually meant that the Church has been able to export and win "clients" in continents outside Europe. Let us take the last hundred years, for example:

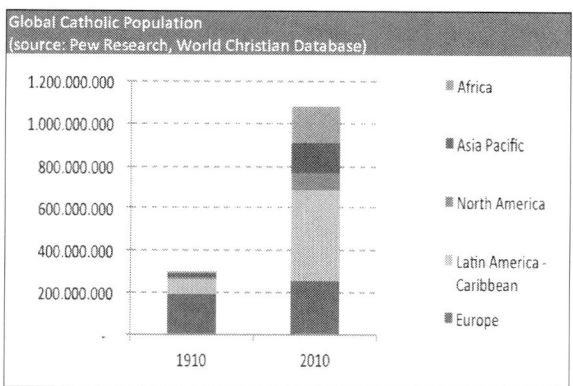

---

[3] A modular pricing model: a version of the product offered free of charge to encourage trial use, while another, more evolved product is sold at full price.

And yet the Church is missing something: the segmentation of its current and potential "clients": this is, I imagine, because the room for growth is seen in the corners of the world in which no competitor has yet taken root: if we exclude Asia, indeed, there are various areas where it is still below what would be considered its "*fair share*[4]" of the market.

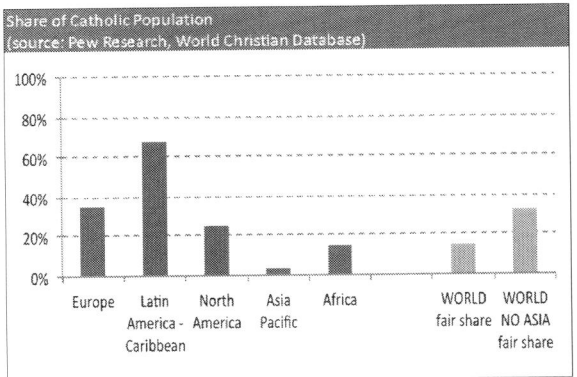

Another fundamental characteristic that has made the Church great, besides the clever use of the four Ps, is the need that it seeks to answer; the need to understand what lies beyond and to know the ways in which to best prepare oneself, which is actually the most relevant thing possible for "clients".

---

[4] Fair Share is the expected market share, and refers to the share that a company should have in each category/area (as in this case), considering that it should have the same share as it has in the entire market of reference.

For every other organisation or company, the work is clearly harder: in the absence of such universal and relevant demand, every company needs to choose what shape to give to the need that it intends to satisfy with its products or services (*marketing insight*[5]), varying it according to the various different market segments available.

Marketing essentially has its origins in this, the aim or necessity that companies have to understand consumers' needs – whether explicit or implicit, functional or emotional – and then direct products and messages towards them.

Previously all the work, so to speak, was left in the hands of consumers themselves: in the absence of strong competition, you just had to talk about the product and the most functional and concrete benefit it brought, and it was buyers themselves that enriched their consumer experience as best they could. Essentially it "was enough" for consumers to aim for the best offer and the product which best met their needs to not be disappointed: the comparison was on the kind of product and how it performed, characteristics in which there was always, or nearly always, a winner, because it was unique, because it was the first, or because it was a big name worldwide. But today, now that the intrinsic qualities of the products made by the different players in the market are fairly similar, and prices are increasingly aggressive, and the product is available everywhere and there are ten or a hundred products meeting the same need, you have to play a much more refined game, carefully choosing what to say to each segment of the market. So you have to understand the market well, pick different consumer moods, identify the needs and talk to each segment in a very focused way. Above all, you have to do it in a very efficient way, because consumers will in any case not want to pay more than a certain amount, because of the strong competition.

In other words, the keys to success in marketing increasingly relate to a firm's capacity to execute intelligence activities on the large amount of data

---

[5] This is an understanding of consumers which can drastically impact a company's sales, if used capably by marketing. It comes from "*in*" and "*sight*", so what is seen inside consumers, not just inside their heads, but – and above all – inside their sentiments and their emotions, which often they themselves don't even manage to express: successful brands are consequently those that manage to understand and communicate consumer insights before, and better, than others.

which is now available, to discover new approaches, those new views on needs to be satisfied, which will represent the real competitive advantage in the market.

I know very well that a lot of people nowadays don't like talking about targets, because it is a term which is often associated with the military and thus based on the idea that there will be a war to be fought, a blow to be launched, prey to be captured, an enemy to be beaten[6]. I too feel that the meaning that has been widely accepted for this term is now obsolete in a context in which the dynamics of choice, of attachment to a brand, of the socialisation of values are a lot closer to the concept of community or tribe, than to that of a sum of individuals, to be aimed at. "From targets to people: there aren't any targets to hit, but rather people with whom to resonate" write Cova, Pallera and Giordano amongst the ten fundamental principles of non-conventional marketing[7].

I also don't like the term "target" because it appears static, something that can be determined once and for all, and which does not reflect the extreme dynamism with which bands of consumers now enter and exit consumer, social or psychological clusters.

However, I wouldn't remove the term "target" from the marketing glossary: "target", with a softer significance and one that relates to its meaning as being an "objective", I believe has still a lot to give and with this meaning still works very well.

Indeed, it is precisely the proliferation of opportunities provided by technological development that pushes a lot of companies from the strategy, from the goals which they are seeking by operating on the market. A lot of companies follow the fashion of the times or the fascinating solutions put forward by trendy agencies, forgetting the original scope of a particular initiative without looking closely at the expected results: but remaining focused on one's own targets, on what counts and on one's own goals, is the only guarantee of effectiveness in such complex markets.

That is why I personally have not given up using the term, but I give it a different meaning. A "target" is thus not something to be aimed at, a group of consumers, but it is the objective, the focus, the lens with which to carry

---

[6] Reference is particularly made to the excellent work on the theory of Post Modern Marketing popularised particularly by B. Cova and G. Fabbris.

[7] *"Non conventional marketing. viral, guerrilla, trival, societing and the ten fundamental principles of post-modern marketing"* 2007, published by Sole 24 Ore

out marketing activities[8]. This is also because over the past twenty years the very concept of target has continued to evolve:

- From audience to target
- From consumer to prosumer
- From client to stakeholder
- From demographic classifications to that of shared values (generations)

---

[8] www.wordreference.com/enit/target

From Audiences to Targets

There are two kinds of marketing: one which is aimed at everybody and one which previously identifies a segment and directs all its messages to that segment. The choice of opting for one kind of marketing or another depends on a series of factors, as well as company culture and capacity: there are companies which because of their mission, or more prosaically just to survive, must necessarily aim at the whole market, and companies which, because of the product type or production capacity, have to aim at smaller numbers.

Companies like the public broadcasters, for example, can only see the whole population as their target market. Company statutes, their mission for the population and the generalist nature of channels don't leave room for creativity: the company has to attract audiences and bring together a very wide band of people, which tends towards the whole population. It doesn't matter what age, sex, geographic provenance, or the preferences of the users are: every consumer is potentially interesting for them; every possible viewer is a target; every user is a citizen on which the company can carry out its mission; every consumer has spending power (direct or indirect for advertising purposes).

Companies like that don't break down into segments: they sell mass-market products, which are often big ticket items and which over time have acquired consumer after consumer until they cover very wide market segments. These include, for example, a lot of banks, transport companies, telephone operators, and food: these are companies that have to speak to everybody.

And yet even this kind of company has now realised that "one size fits all" marketing doesn't work any more, since it is a compromise, which follows an average consumer who in reality doesn't actually exist, because the world now stresses individualism and promises everyone that it will satisfy their needs and requirements, in a unique and personalised way. Because of this, the most advanced companies tend to differentiate by product line, moving from mass marketing (or average marketing) to marketing by segments, which means reaching the same market coverage through the sum of business generated by various different products.

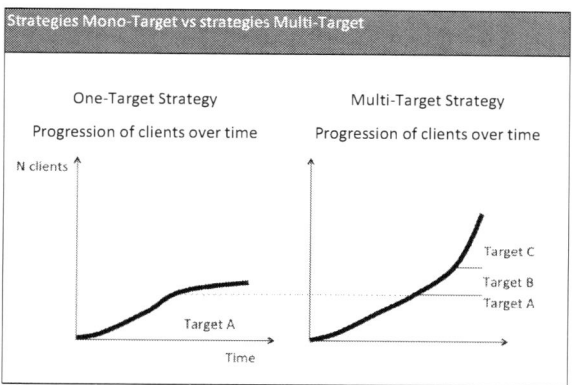

It is now that we pass from an audience logic, to that of a target logic: direct marketing to an audience seeks to reach the maximum number of consumers possible within a given socio-demographic characteristic (potential consumers are young people, adults, women or men); whereas marketing based on targets identifies different needs within those potential audiences and plans specific activities, using an incremental logic.

There are many ways to define a target, and this text doesn't aim to show all of them in detail. Some of the various ways relate to socio-demographic, value and cultural segmentation: all of which are effective ways to describe, identify and work on consumer segments starting from their needs and their personal characteristics.

From Consumer to Prosumer[9]

The company produces, consumers buy. The company sells the products it knows how to make, consumers buy the products that they want. It is the law of demand and supply which we have all studied: there are two kinds of operator in a market, those who sell and those who buy.

Then new consumers arrive: people who play with the brands, modify products, reinvent advertising and publish it on their social media channels. New consumers essentially assemble, or even produce, what they buy.

They look very odd to marketing directors from Generation X who grew up in the 80s with brands and consumerism: years in which a brand was a status symbol, which showed that you belonged to a group, perhaps that you had made it after sacrifice and saving. For those reasons, brands were sacrosanct: people wanted something, and owned it; they showed off, and got respect and admiration. People bought something because everyone did, because it was famous.

But Millennials look for niche brands, or ask better known brands to be "open" and to make personalised rather than mass market products. They grew up with every solution to hand, focusing every decision process on themselves: Millennial consumers don't choose the best option amongst those available, but themselves create the option that best meets their needs. New consumers configure their product or service, and interpret it by modifying the base structure, mixing elements with others from competing products and in some cases are even likely to reach the company's production processes. That is why we talk of "co-creation": a production process which includes the interaction between producer and consumer in putting together products or services.

There are now a lot of companies which have started to indulge consumer requests, by making available:
- customisable products, in terms of combining base elements from the same product with a free configuration approach;

---

[9] Term coined in 1980 by the futurologist Alvin Toffler in his book *"The Third Wave"*.

- products that were created to be customised by the client after purchase;
- products that have shared usage (*sharing economy*);
- products created by other consumers.

Millennial consumers are almost never consumers: they don't often limit themselves to using what other people produce – they do that only if the product category doesn't interest them – but rather they more often take action relating to the product before (by choosing it), during (configuring it) or after it is manufactured (customising it).

Selling to this kind of consumer isn't easy for a company that has been conceived and structured for scalable mass production. It is easier for service companies, even though infrastructure and cultural issues often restrict theoretical possibilities, but in the world of manufacturing companies this means a drastic change in the production system, logistics and distribution, and also in the way marketing is done. In fact communicating with a consumer means giving up communicating about the product and its benefits. It also means giving up communicating about adhering to a lifestyle. Marketing aimed at prosumers is collaborative marketing, which makes available a service that benefits what the consumer will later do, as if they were two parts of the same production chain.

According to this concept of clients, the target is not thus thought of as someone who will consume our product, but somebody who will use it for reasons not known to us previously. Those who aim their product offering to a prosumer target make their assets and know-how available: in some way they activate, facilitate and empower the consumer.

How do we find this kind of consumer? They will make themselves known... if indeed the reputation of our company in some particular area of know-how is good, they themselves will know how to come and knock on our door: it will be them who become the first fans of our Facebook page, them to talk about the brand in the various online communities, them to write e-mails and tweet suggestions on the various aspects of company management, from how to do PR to suggestions for new products.

So the step from thinking of targets as "consumers" to thinking of them as "prosumers" requires a serious listening and opening approach.

From Client to Stakeholder

In the previous section, the company target became a consumer that is also in part a producer (prosumer); in this section, we will put forward another version of this.

With the increase in general awareness of sustainability and social responsibility issues, a company's target grows to include all those individuals who are potentially impacted by what the firm does, in terms of cultural and social development, as well as the economic development of the community where it operates. So it is not just the consumers of the brand that call for good conduct from it.

The spread of digitalisation and the strength of word of mouth through social media has actually made companies vulnerable to consumer communities which, together with – and often even before and in greater number than – institutions, impose correct behaviour from a range of points of view: respecting promises made on product performance is a key point in the relationship, but companies are also assessed for the accuracy of their communication, ethical conduct, and their financial solidity. It is thus no longer enough to offer a good product and attractive marketing: according to this concept of target, we ought to pay attention to the various different manifestations of our conduct, considering all those with possible interests (stakeholders) as our targets.

A stakeholder is more than a consumer, and is more than a client: stakeholders are subjects who are part of the community in which the company operates, or with which the company has direct or indirect links, associated with the products that they consume or otherwise. The more a company has an impact on the economic, social and cultural situation of individuals, the more its relationship with people can be independent of whether they consume the product or not. The success of a company depends on the relationship that it sets up in the environment in which it operates or which it might have an impact upon: we should think about the consequences of relationship issues, about the HR strategies one company follows, about the goodwill gained by a particular brand that produces goods following rules that favour the local community. Essentially, we should think about the possibility one has of choosing to become or not become a consumer of a certain product because of the social values that the brand adopts and promotes.

This interpretation of targets clearly requires, amongst other things, quite a substantial internal transformation of the company, a new concept of the role of marketing itself: no longer just trying to get to know the needs of consumers and direct their product offering accordingly, but with a much wider perimeter, which starts from the needs of individuals in their community without just considering them in terms of being a consumer.

Unfortunately companies are still traditionally divided up into sealed compartments to be able to buy into this vision of consumers, but some examples are beginning to appear: cross-functional groups are being set up (from marketing to PR, and as far as R&D and financial departments) to work on wide-ranging projects, which stem from the awareness that success in the market is very closely linked to reputation and to the population group of reference[10].

In other words, if marketing initiatives are inspired by a target seen as a stakeholder, companies will no longer have to come up with a campaign to convince consumers to buy a product or consume more of it, but rather will have to aim their marketing at creating engagement with a given individual or community. The final goal of a company is obviously sales and profit, so things must necessarily tend in that direction, but the way in which it will be achieved will be profoundly different. After defining its mission to the community (*purpose*), or the *raison d'être* inside the interest system (social, ethical, economic interests, etc.), the aims towards consumers-stakeholders will be very different from a simplistic "selling more": the company will set itself a goal of influencing a change in the consumer which can bring him or her benefits, and consequently also the company itself.

If we were to talk about a soft drinks company, for example, the task for marketing would no longer be to increase brand awareness or to convince people that it is better, better looking and healthier than the competitor's. But rather, for example, to change the way in which people approach the product category, or get people to think when they drink, or make them reflect on the fact that every drink has a given meaning. Done like that, the company will create engagement with its consumers-stakeholders, who will thus sign up for a lifestyle and not to a product on the market.

---

[10] The Barilla campaign is a good example of this: "Good for you, good for the Planet" www.goodforyougoodfortheplanet.org

This different way of thinking of one's priority interlocutor, changing them from consumer to stakeholder, creates a series of implications on which to base the way in which the target itself is identified, understood and involved. One of the most consolidated techniques used in this area, after having mapped the stakeholders and with awareness of the different kinds of handling which are normal to each segment (consumer, journalist, association, employee, etc and whatever it may be), relates to the method with which one can pass from the concept of consumer to that of *Personas (persons)*. Identifying targets with the *personas* technique means describing them using archetypal features which suggest some type of individual in a clear and immediate way. They are viewed in a rounded way, and not just in terms of their particular attitudes, consumption preferences or use of resources.

These techniques mean one can set targets that are broader and deeper: satisfying somebody means entering their life, understanding their history and what is important to them, and leads to understanding what role one can give oneself inside the much larger system of inputs that the subject receives for their satisfaction, pleasure, self-realisation and – why not? - happiness. It is worth noting that marketing is not interested in the personal lives of their subjects, but is rather interested in that part of their lives that is looked at through the "lens" of the marketer. It is interesting for marketers to understand how their aims can be reached by working with how individuals express their human behaviour and interests.

Finally, to make the communication of the target to the company's teams and consultants even more incisive, the description of the "person" is enriched with soft elements such as name, age, place of origin, profession and so on so as to add still more anchors to the reality in which the target lives.

In this case too, we can't write exhaustively about this idea of "personas" so as not to make the text too long, and so we recommend one of the cornerstone texts on the issue, *"The Inmates Are Running the Asylum"*, written by Alan Cooper in 1998.

Generations as segments in marketing

After this quick round-up of some contemporary variations on the concept of target, which are often dictated by emerging consumption styles, we look at the issue of segmentation from the perspective of this book. Generations can inspire communication and marketing initiatives which are far more articulate than those based purely on age or gender. This is because shared values are at their core and can allow companies to focus on those shared motivational forces to drive consumer choices.

A generation as such is usually focussed upon from varying angles or viewpoints (including marketing) when the market segment is still very young. That's obvious, since sociologists and psychologists begin to talk of a generation as soon as they detect new psychological, social and cultural currents in the population and that happens when "new" young people with different behavioural patterns, and approaches to life, or different values are noticed. An individual's value system and their peer group is actually formed at a young age, and never when they are old. That is why we talk so much of a generation when they are young, just as soon as they appear.

Social Study flow

A. New Values born in society

B. A new Generation begins

C. This will be the population of the future

D. We study the youth today to understand what the future will look like

This is essentially the equation of this book: we talk about young people because we are talking about a new generation; we are talking about a new generation because we are talking about a new system of values which we have to take into account, including marketing.

A generation is actually not just a group of individuals born at a specific time: a generation is a group of individuals who, having been impacted at the same stage of life by a technological, economic, social or cultural revolution, have changed their value system from those of preceding generations. In other words, a generation is defined by how the future is seen and the ideals that are shared, and not simply by the age.

Consequently, communicating with a generation means communicating considering the values in which they believe, and on the basis on which they differentiate themselves from others from those of the past.

Social Study flow VS Marketing Study flow	
A. New Values born in society	A. We study youth and I compared them with previous ones
B. A new Generation begins	B. We understand that a new generation began
C. This will be the population of the future	C. We understand their values
D. We study the youth today to understand what the future will look	D. We understand implications for marketing

We can say that there are essentially six generations which have been the subject of marketing in various ways and levels of intensity:
- **Lost Generation**: those born towards the end of the 19th century.
- **Greatest Generation**: those born at the beginning of the 20th century.
- **Silent Generation**: those born between the 1920s and the beginning of the 1940s.

- **Baby Boomers**: those born after the Second World War, between the beginning of the 1940s and the beginning of the 1960s.
- **Generation X**: those born between the second half of the 1960s and the beginning of the 1980s.
- **Millennials and Centennials** (or Generation Y and Z): those born between the mid-1980s and the end of the 1990s, together with those born afterwards (Centennials or Post-Millennials).

In the next chapter we will look more closely at marketing techniques and approaches aimed at recent generations: to anticipate this, I would like to mention some Coca-Cola slogans that have been used over the years and which I find especially significant in the history of that company and the way it has accompanied the history of consumers themselves through the various generations[11]:

```
1886 - Drink Coca-Cola
1904 - Delicious and Refreshing
1917 - Three Million a Day
1922 - Thirst Knows No Season
1923 - Enjoy Thirst
1924 - Refresh Yourself
1925 - Six Million a Day
1927 - Around the Corner from Everywhere
1938 - The Best Friend Thirst Ever Had
1942 - The Only Thing Like Coca-Cola is Coca-Cola Itself
1948 - Where There's Coke There's Hospitality
1952 - What You Want is a Coke
1956 - Coca-Cola... Makes Good Things Taste Better
1963 - Things Go Better with Coke
1969 - It's the Real Thing
1971 - I'd Like to Buy the World a Coke
1979 - Have a Coke and a Smile
1982 - Coke Is It!
1985 - America's Real Choice (for Coca-Cola and Coca-Cola classic)
1987 - When Coca-Cola is a Part of Your Life, You Can't Beat the Feeling
1993 - Always Coca-Cola
2000 - Coca-Cola. Enjoy
2005 - Make It Real
2009 - Open Happiness
```

---

[11] The complete sequence of Coca-Cola advertising slogans was put on the company website in 2014 at www.coca-colaitalia.it/storie/storia-degli-slogan-pubblicitari-coca-cola

Cap. II – WHAT WE HAVE EXPERIENCED: BABY BOOMERS AND GENERATION X

Baby Boomer Marketing: needs, values and expectations

They were born in the two decades between 1945 and 1964. The "Baby Boomer" name refers to the boom in births which occurred in the US and in several other countries in the west after the Second World War. Couples celebrated the end of war – and the associated time of economic crisis and social uncertainty – with the most resounding greeting for the future: "*The cry of the baby was heard across the land*" wrote the historian Landon Jones in reference to those years.

People from that generation are older than fifty, and the oldest are around 75 years old. To understand them we have to analyse the world in which they grew up and the impact that this has had on their habits and aspirations since they were young: children of parents that had suffered the Great Depression of 1929 and the subsequent World War were young people with great hope. So it is a generation which grew up with the idea of being able to live in a world that was moving forward, which was to become more prosperous and better than it was in the past.

When young, the Baby Boomers lived in the era of "the Miracle", "the Dream", the time of economic growth which took place after the war in several western countries, between the 1950s and 1970s. Children and adolescents grew up in comfortable, nice houses, as part of families which were enthusiastic about their new purchases: splendid, new, branded products, fridges, washing machines and televisions and a nice car became symbols of a higher standard of living, which was primarily ensured by job security.

Growing up in such a world automatically created a generation which was very confident, and which focused on independence and had strong professional and social aspirations: these are some of the aspects that most characterise Baby Boomers. Amongst the values that this generation have in common in most of the Western Countries is the wish to achieve wellbeing and independence through a satisfied and settled family. This was often also a consequence of consumption.

The Baby Boomers were young between the 1970s and 80s. More precisely, in 1975 the youngest was ten and the "oldest" was actually thirty, just like our Centennials and Millennials.

We are putting together the values of the Baby Boomer generation through a collection of basic concepts which describe their unique character:

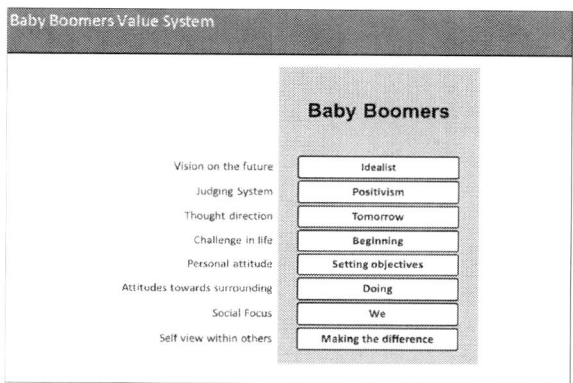

So what was marketing like at that time, around 1975? It was marketing that in 1976 said "*Coke Adds Life*" and three years later "*Have a Coke and a Smile*". It was marketing that spoke to them, the young people of the time: positive, wanting fun and dreams, with much better prospects than their parents had.

In this boom time scenario, the function of marketing was to understand - and to set in action – the stimuli with which to attract consumers who were concerned about moving up the social ladder, as big or small as it was for each of them. **Information on products and what they offered were enriched by communication on** benefits which enthused people even more, like **joy, youth, social prestige**: brands took on the role of status symbols.

A brand meant quality, but most of all happiness, success, freedom, independence, self confidence and prestige: from logos to advertising, these are the values of the target that marketing interpreted and communicated with its products.

All the elements cited above can also be found in advertising:

Generation X Marketing: needs, values, expectations

It's never easy to write about one's own generation, and perhaps it isn't even the right thing to do: we often get caught up in our own experiences and in the stereotypes of us that we ourselves have participated in creating, as we look to make the icons of our time immortal.

In the same way it isn't easy for marketing directors from Generation X to give up the stimuli and the ways that contributed to the greatness of the brands that were symbols of their youth, and take on a new world: we often look at today's young people as if they were similar to the young people of the 1980s.

Generation X is made up of those born between the sixties and the beginning of the eighties: I am one of them, as I was born in 1973. The world that hosted me when I was a teenager was that of the 80s to 90s: at that stage the oldest members of Generation X was not much over twenty, while the youngest was the same age as Generation Z today.

While the Cold War between the US and the USSR hung over us and cast a shadow of doubt on the future, on what was to happen and on the ability that we had as individuals, realistically, of changing our world, the world worked out its own idea of who to back. In a lot of western countries the US won the competition. The conjunction of the sense of expectation between what could happen (the Third World War) and the pro-American line culminated in the *Yuppies* movement: Young Urban Professionals ("yuppie") is that term coined in the early 80s which represents the cultural phenomenon behind the need of appearance of this generation. These were young people looking to express themselves within the confines of the cocoon-like world of the popular – often from the "winning" America - brands or were inspired by it: the world surrounding them was an environment from which taking opportunities or chances to fly, to grow, to desire something.

At the same time, the birth of the commercial television companies in several European Countries became the alternative to public televisions, spread the idea of being able to enjoy the most modern and entertaining content without charge thanks to advertising: brands enabled people to satisfy their wish to escape, and to dream. In summary the laissez-faire and consumerist American culture of that time, which was in contrast to the grey and rigid world of the 1970s petrol crisis, spoke to the youth of the time giving them an aspirational world in which to believe and even to take refuge in.

X Generation World

This came in a technological context which had a strong impact on this generation giving them all the tools to believe in and put into practice their own egocentricism. It is worth reflecting on some of the inventions of those times:
- the walkman (1980)
- the personal computer (1980)
- the CD reader (1982)
- the cellphone (1983)
- the world wide web (1989)

A number of these inventions opened the way to today's developments, in that they gave users the possibility of creating content enjoying it unrestrictedly, in an individual way.

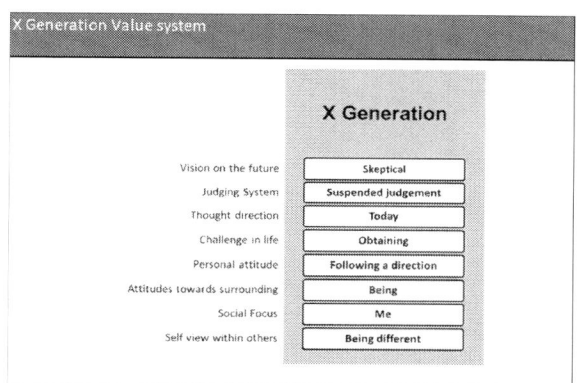

1980s and 1990s marketing stressed advertising as a stimulus above all others, and sought to publicise brands as much as possible, just as the big American brands, from Coca-Cola to Nike did at the time. Advertising could be done without any more links to the past, by conversing with people who were strongly aligned with the aims of the advertising client, which was to sell. Consumers were extraordinarily reactive: spending on advertising in the various media available guaranteed results in terms of awareness and sales.

The brand, for its part, had to set itself the goal of **showing an ideal world, perhaps an escapist one, a kind of chance for consumers**, and asserted itself to them, even if with a light and carefree tone.

Brands made great use of family stereotypes and often sought refuge in parodies of common sense which at the end of the day had **the aim of reaffirming identity and a sense of belonging**, in a world that saw a harshening of conflict in several different areas: the geo-political conflict between the US and the USSR, the domestic struggle between political parties, the commercial battles between brand products and even those unknown ones, between Coca-Cola and Pepsi Cola, between Nike and Adidas, between one and the contrary. The most successful brand names of the eighties stressed areas of aggregation, providing aspirational worlds in which Generation X recognised itself. Generation X grew up in a world dominated by oppositions and consumers were born with this mindset: when they used to be young, they were loyal, they belonged to something, they did not belong to the opposite, they judged products, brands and advertising for what they meant but also – and often – for what they don't.

X Generation - Advertising
Image, Belonging, Escapism

Cap. III –WHERE WE ARE NOW: THE MILLENNIAL BANG

Who Millennials are

The term "Millennial" is not the synonym of "young person" used by marketing people, who are always looking for a new label, preferably in English, to give to the things they are working on: it is a specific generation and not a simple demographic segment that we can find in every era. Because of this, a Millennial will always be such, even aged 50: in other words, if the segmentation of the Millennials is adopted, it is a choice to segment a group of individuals who have the same values and ideas in common and not just an age range.

What defines Millennials is the technological, social and cultural revolution experienced since they were adolescents with the move from the Web 1.0 to the so-called Web 2.0: it is a digital ecosystem which is radically newer than its predecessor, which has brought with it a different way of experiencing the Internet, characterised by a high level of interaction with websites and the consequent spread of thought, opinions, movements and ideas between people.

A lot of people feel this is a genuine revolution, a moment of technological evolution which breaks with the past and, compared to it, makes a leap forward which is so important as to change society: the way that people inter-relate, behavioural rules, the way in which information spreads, the rites, values and icons around which a new culture make up an untried framework. Millennials are young people who have grown up at a time when all of this was starting out, when the Web 1.0 changed into the Web 2.0.

Specifically they are those young people who saw the Web 2.0 as adolescents and have experienced it before anything else: they were pioneers who didn't have the option of making comparisons with others, they are now young under-35s, for whom a limited and uncertain future is often forecast. These are teenagers from 2004-2009, who have dealt with their personal and social growth at the same time that the Web 2.0 was starting out and establishing itself throughout the world.

When they asked themselves about – and established – their own identity, or when they wondered about their future and what they wanted to be, they did so using social networks, blogs, forums, and compared ideas, opportunities and products with thousands of other young people of the same age, all around the world. That is why they are so different from the generations which preceded them: they are the first generation which, thanks to social media and to the chance of exploring, comparing and socialising, has really grown up free, open, informed and global.

Seen from this view of globalisation, they are unique: people born before them lived their youth in environments that were - by comparison – too small, too slow, and too analogical; those born later, like the Centennials, will live in a world which has already been "new" for a bit, with older kids who are able to understand, help, explain and warn either directly or through their mistakes.

To sum up, this generation has emerged because of the Web 2.0, and has grown up with it, from 2004 onwards. We are of course using 2004, as a point of reference since that was the year when Tim O' Reilly coined the term Web 2.0 and cited it in an O'Reilly Media conference. Millennials are therefore the adolescents of those years, young people then aged no more than twenty. People now in their early forties were already no longer adolescents at that time and so were not impacted by technology in the same way: they were 26-28 years old then, already grown up, with a well-shaped identity, perhaps they already held down a job, and technology – although revolutionary in a lot of areas – didn't work on their psychology and sociability in the way that it did the adolescents of that time. Every child and teenager of the post-Millennium period, dealing with their individual and social growth, was decisively impacted by technological, connected systems.

If thus we want to provide some dated reference points, to accompany the sociological definition with the one of a demographic nature, which is much more used in marketing, we can define Millennials as those born from the middle of the 1980s onwards: they are the young people who as this is being written are aged between 20 and 34. The Centennials are young people who were born after this, they are today's teenagers and are aged under twenty.

So first of all they have been able to build their own identity and their own relationship system in a really untried way, compared with what happened in the past:
- they have discovered the possibility of writing a blog and they have seen that it is read by people all over the world;

- they have looked for information on a forum and have appreciated other people's altruism in giving good advice;
- they have modified how history is told, changing an entry on Wikipedia;
- they have really felt that they are friends with hundreds of people they don't know, by sharing an interest, a passion, or an idea.

And with companies?
- they have posted an advertising campaign on their Facebook profile and seen the number of "likes" and "shares" grow, making it become viral in just a few weeks; they have modified, dubbed, parodied and derided another campaign on YouTube, and got hundreds of thousands of views in just a few hours;
- they derided a celebrity spokesperson to the point where they saw the firm change the person used in their advertising;
- they chose the logo of a brand for their profile and destroyed another because the product didn't get delivered on time, or was different from what shown on the website;
- they have developed friendships with companies, have asked questions, received answers and got customised gifts.

Let's be clear: the delirium of omnipotence which is typical of adolescence has found an outlet in relationships with brands!

All this actually relates to the possibility, the capacity and desire of these kids to give and receive feedback and opinions: that is one of the fundamental aspects in defining the Millennial generation. It is precisely the visibility and sharing of their value systems, thanks to continual communication of opinions, which defines and strengthens this generation's sense of belonging. An opinion puts a prospect at the centre of attention, makes information come alive, making it warm and useful. And an exchange of opinions creates a strong link between people: it is transparency, it is a sign of trust, it is a stimulus to growth, it is openness; and all of these are fundamental aspects for Millennials. That is why this generation is more united than others, even though it doesn't express itself in social struggles or "established" movements: it has unveiled itself and sees itself in the way in which it still tackles and deals with the Web 2.0.

The skills acquired from living in these informed and interconnected worlds has an implication for anyone who does marketing: power relations are much more equal, like those between friends. The gap between companies and consumers, between those who create information and those who read it, between teachers and students, between doctor and patient, between seller and buyer, has become increasingly narrow. And the different positions are now the subject of a significant reflection: companies and institutions (in a wide sense) are looking for new roles in the relationship with their interlocutors.

Another implication of growing up in these connected worlds is the capacity to create – quickly and effectively – interest groups around individual contents, interests, goals or projects. The lynchpin around which these groups of Millennials revolve is almost never a person, a place, a fixed point; it is the very goal of getting together which is itself the driver and stimulus, even without significant effort or promotion. The group's mission, we could say, takes the place of the hero. It is a "pull" way of coming together as a group, and no longer a "push" way: it is the content, the passion which, since its nature is to lack an owner, sponsor or leader, attracts and brings people together as a group.

Visibility and exchange of opinion is thus a determining factor in understanding this generation and the relationship that it seeks to have with other people, including companies: those who have grown up with this imprinting, on the one hand ask for a frank and transparent relationship, in the interest of both parties; on the other they ask for something relevant to talk about, perhaps even to argue about, and to share. "Feedback" and "Content" are the two foundation stones of Post Millennial Marketing, of which we will talk at greater length later.

Given that a lot of today's marketing directors are part of Generation X, please allow me a further focus on the fundamental differences between Generation X and Generation Y. To this end I am including a passage from "Generazione 2.0. Chi sono cosa vogliono, come dialogare con loro", in which Millennials and Generation X are compared:

"They didn't live through the fall of the Berlin Wall (they had only just been born), but they have heard the broken dreams of those young people. They didn't suffer from the psychological damage of the Cold War, but they lived through the pitiless 2003 Gulf War, which was often viewed by

television news as the story of a necessary act, but one full of contradictions and stage management. They didn't have positive parents who grew up during the economic boom years, but ones who were actually disorientated, at the mercy of the collapse in confidence in the institutions, politics and western technological economy. When they were small they didn't watch cartoons in which it was always the good guy that won, but instead played video games in which the only thing that counted was skill, with no guarantee of a happy ending.

Nor did they live through the eighties, which were years of show, nor the nineties, which were ones of individualism. But they did live through the 2000s, which began with the attack on the Twin Towers. It was the time of a reality check, and globalisation.

To summarise, it is a generation born from the ashes of the certainties of the preceding generations, which grew up in a world of abrupt changes; between something impossible that actually happens, and certainties that

evaporate in an instant, it is a generation that is accustomed to steer between what is real, surreal and virtual in any circumstance, from the most everyday ones, to those linked to important occurrences in the political situation.

Just as in "Big Brother", the television format that has been the most watched of this generation, the reality show in which it is never revealed what belongs to reality and what to fiction."

The Post-Millennials or Centennials

If Millennials grew up with social media, leaving behind the "old" world of the Web 1.0 to open the doors to the Web 2.0, the Centennials don't even have an idea of what happened in the time between one and the other. At least Millennials had parents, older brothers and sisters, teachers who talked to them about it, still linked to fixed points and the physical world... Centennials were born into the connected world and don't have any memory of the move between on and off-line, between Web 1.0 and Web 2.0, between desktop and mobile usage of a connected device, between the content shown from a TV or a cell phone. The fact that they haven't seen the past will perhaps save them from those who at all costs seek to remember the world as it was to reaffirm their own identity, including in marketing.

The Centennials, not having lived through the passage between the two "worlds", don't have conflicts to resolve or causes to back: they can have an impartial vision of things, assessing the real and the virtual, 1.0 and 2.0, old and (no longer) new, in a balanced way. Now there is even research from which a characteristic of this generation emerges with a certain coherence: the awareness and the balance of knowing how to reconcile on and off-line, without passion, theoretical points of view, or fascination.

To look for a similar case, let's recall what happened with the cultural revolution in '68. A generation imposed new cultural and social values by destroying the rules and values which had been recognised up to that time: daughters answered their mothers back, and questioned their complete dedication to the family; sons questioned the zealous severity of their fathers; students questioned teaching methods; citizens questioned unfounded policies and pre-established power. There was a before and they wanted an after. The world that the 68-ers dreamed of was necessarily an idealised one: you had to fly very high to be able to detach oneself and challenge the world. The same thing happened to Millennials: they have completely embraced the world they experience in social media, contrasting it to the real world and the constraints that, by necessity, it placed.

They actually grew up[12]:

- **without geographic constraints**, since content availability was immediate, even if it was produced on the other side of the world;
- **without time constraints**, since content was born, died and returned online without a continuous flow;
- **without constraints on communication**, because they talked, wrote and posted all kinds of things, with everybody, in all possible ways;
- **without any on-off**, because they were always "on" and never "off";
- **without privacy**, because the Internet and businesses hosted them, providing room for expression without which it had become impossible to live and socialise;
- **without limits on quantity**, because they could get everything, without charge, immediately, without having to choose between specified options.
- **without things**, because they were interested in use and not ownership, the thing in itself was not interesting, but rather the service and specific benefit connected to it.

The 68-ers and Millennials share the revolutionary nature of things and the wish to change and to flee from the constraints and limits which they felt they were subjected to, even though the former group probably didn't have the chance to make their values shared right across their generation.

These similarities lead us to better understand what to expect from the Centennials. Those who came after '68 have viewed critically the ways in which young people from that time have made their ideas progress, and have tried to keep from that time the most positive values, blunting the roughness and the idealism. The Centennials will do the same thing with the Millennials' idealised world: they experience the digital world, but know that even the analogical world of the past had some benefits – they can assess if and when one is better than another, they can observe and choose. They don't need to impose a "without", but can assess what is better and most useful without dogmas, they can obtain one, the other, or both.

---

[12] Refer to the "Less is More Generation" chapter of *"#Generazione 2.0"op. cit.*, for further explanation of the concept.

I have two children, one born in 2008 and another in 2013, and I can confess that it is a real hoot seeing them and us together. It is often them who ask my wife and I not to look at our smartphones! But other times they ask us to play with one of the apps that they are obsessed with together with them. Other times we really feel embarrassed to see that they can't keep still without an iPad.... So all in all, Centennials are not black or white, and they are definitively not fully digital, as we probably expected. They are everything, and often everything together.

It is perhaps too early to describe the Centennials as a generation. We should wait for them to grow up a bit to understand the values that they will take forward and their idea of the future, but we can already state some things about them. **Generation Z** (or Centennials, to be clear), if it has a value compared with Millennials, it **will be precisely the value of the awareness** of the balance between on and offline, with the consequent pragmatism and practical sense: the sharpest observers, those who don't want to make the news, and who don't follow stereotypes, are converging on what may potentially be their characteristic.

Millennials are the recipients of values that are very important and "high minded" such as health globalisation, freedom of thought and expression, collaboration and co-creation, independence of brands and advertising. All of us have the responsibility of helping them to create this world, but a risk is already clear: that they are a bit too far away from the world of today, that they come from the analogical world, which is old and gerontocratic but which houses them, to be able to react and really change the ground rules of our society and – as far as this book is concerned – to change the paradigms of marketing.

Whereas Generation Z, which is set for a reality check, could be the one which, perhaps by coming down a step, takes advantage of these values, and adopts the most concrete, everyday, obtainable and real version of them. That is why the popularity of platforms like Snapchat is exploding to the detriment of Facebook itself, which is what Millennials grew up with: they are social networks that allow a conversation that lasts the time of a joke... and as a result – which seems paradoxical – is true. If things can disappear, they must be true and free of frills, not like in Facebook, where what is claimed is often an exaggeration of reality. Let us say it again, what if what happened to the 68-ers and successive generations were to repeat itself? Somebody sowed the seeds, aiming for an ideal world that could never have been completely made, but others will reap.

At the end of this digression on the values of Generations Y and Z, we put together the character of the Millennials (and Post Millennials) through the same system of concepts used by other generations:

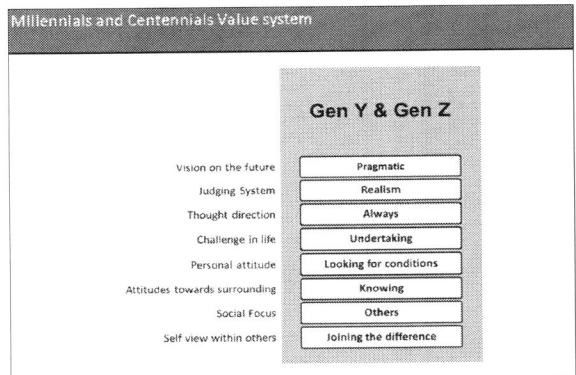

Millennials and Centennials in figures

From a marketing point of view, a segment deserves attention (or investments to understand it, and to "make it a target") if it is numerous or if it has value, or it generates sales for the firm through direct or indirect purchases.

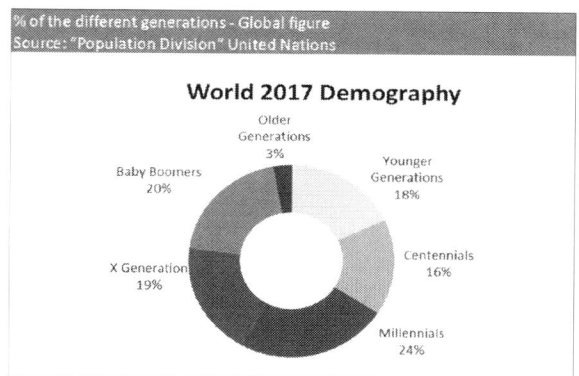

Let us begin with the first point: how many Millennials are there? Are there a lot of them or a just a few? Clearly that is a question which calls for a relative and not an absolute answer, or: how many of them are there in comparison to my total number of potential buyers/consumers? If my brand or product is strategically aimed at an audience of young people, well then by definition there are really a lot of Millennials, since they will be the totality of my consumers. However if we go beyond that specific case, some part of the world can only view a young target as being highly relevant, since it represents the largest segment of the population in question.

Let's look at the figures in detail[13]:

Location	Total Population (000)	% Youngers	% Centennials + Millennials	Centennials + Millennials Population (000)	% Olders
World	7,349,469	18%	40%	2,961,888	42%
Africa	1,186,177	39%	46%	546,249	26%
Eastern Africa	394,477	37%	46%	167,500	22%
Middle Africa	155,982	38%	45%	69,947	21%
Northern Africa	223,890	23%	44%	97,971	33%
Southern Africa	62,833	27%	47%	29,647	32%
Western Africa	353,824	21%	46%	161,284	25%
Asia	4,393,297	87%	41%	1,790,769	43%
Eastern Asia	1,612,285	11%	35%	558,508	54%
South-Central Asia	1,889,288	20%	45%	853,911	35%
South-Eastern Asia	633,491	18%	42%	267,192	40%
Western Asia	257,033	27%	44%	113,215	35%
Europe	738,442	16%	30%	221,192	39%
Eastern Europe	292,984	11%	32%	93,014	57%
Northern Europe	102,357	12%	31%	31,828	57%
Southern Europe	152,042	15%	27%	41,047	61%
Western Europe	190,783	12%	29%	55,304	61%
Latin America and the Caribbean	634,384	18%	42%	268,972	41%
Caribbean	43,197	17%	40%	17,363	43%
Central America	172,741	19%	44%	76,778	37%
South America	418,446	18%	42%	174,854	42%
Northern America	357,839	12%	34%	120,151	54%
Canada	35,942	11%	32%	11,435	57%
United States of America	321,774	13%	34%	108,675	54%
Oceania	39,331	16%	37%	14,555	47%
Australia/New Zealand	28,448	11%	34%	9,691	53%
Melanesia	9,622	28%	46%	4,406	30%
Micronesia	527	20%	43%	224	38%
Polynesia	684	22%	42%	295	38%

One person in four in the world is a Millennial (24%, or around 1.8 billion individuals) and 16% are Centennials (1.2 billion)[14]: in general it is a segment with a lot of people. In some parts of our planet, moreover, young

---

[13] Source: "2015 Revision of World Population Prospects", of the Population Division of the United Nation's Department of Economic and Social Affairs (https://esa.un.org/unpd/wpp)

[14] Let's recall: Millennials were born between the mid 1980s and the second half of the 1990s; Centennials were born after the end of the 1990s and the first decade of the 2000s. For these analyses we consider Millennials as the segment that is now aged between 20 and 34 (born between 1983 and 1997) and Centennials those who are between 10 and 19 (born between 1998 and 2007). Defining a generation in such a specific way is never simple nor is it always a good idea from a sociological point of view, but is often necessary to carry out quantitative analyses which, for obvious reasons, have to identify some precise age brackets.

people are the largest age range amongst the population: in Africa they are 46% of the population (500 million people), in Latin and Central America they are 42% of the population (270 million people) and in Asia they are 41%, as many as 1.8 billion people! In these continents, which have a very different demographic distribution from what we have in the West, the Millennials issue doesn't exist, as under-35s are the reference group.

Besides groupings by geographical area, another very interesting analysis can be done by working out the penetration of the various different generations in the countries with the highest GDPs in the world[15].

---

[15] Source: World Bank, 2015 GDP estimates
(http://data.worldbank.org/indicator/NY.GDP.MKTP.CD)

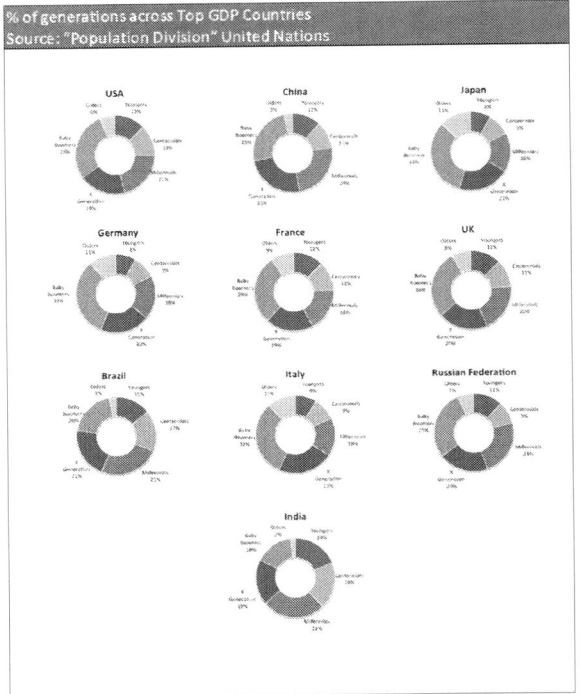

Amongst the countries that make up the Top 10 GDP rankings, only European countries (Germany, France, UK and Italy) show a presence of young people that is less than 33%, while for other countries these generations represent at least a third of the living population. Overall, between Millennials and Centennials, young people are 45% of the populations with highest GDP (the top 10), and are 1.7 billion individuals!

The value of Generations Y and Z are shown below in absolute terms:

Country	Rank GDP	% Centennials	% Millennials	Millennials + Centennials Population (%)	Millennials + Centennials Population (.000)
USA	1				
China	2				
Japan	3				
Germany	4				
France	5				
United Kingdom	6				
Brazil	7				
Italy	8				
Russian Federation	9				
India	10				
Canada	11				
Australia	19				
Spain	13				
Mexico	14				
Republic of Korea	15				
Indonesia	16				
Turkey	17				
Netherlands	18				
Saudi Arabia	19				
Switzerland	20				

As to the issue of the importance of these figures, they tell us how important this generation is, not just for developing countries but also for high-GDP countries.

Amongst the countries with the lowest percentage of young people on the planet, is unfortunately, should I say, as an Italian Italy. Together with Japan, Italy is the oldest country in the world:

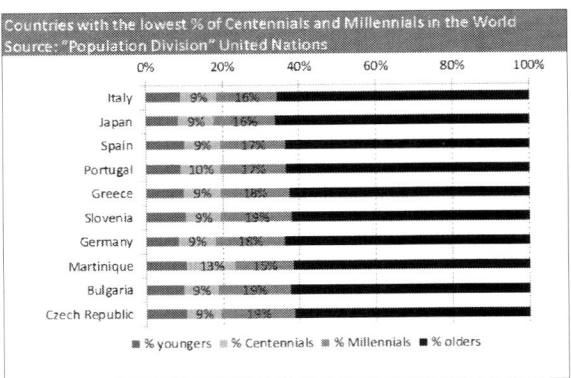

So how can it be that in countries like Italy, Japan, Spain, Portugal, Greece, Slovenia and Germany, that Millennials are talked about so much in advertising agency and company meeting rooms? One thing is clear: understanding how to keep these young people happy is important to prepare ourselves for the future. However many or few are, Millennials and Centennials are tomorrow's consumers.

I once attended a conference and a well known speaker, the CEO of a great multinational company in FMCG, told the audience to be very careful about this "Millennial obsession", as he called it. Our population is ageing and the senior targets represent the main source of our business, today and, even more, in the future. He showed a progression of age groups in time, underling the penetration of older consumers compared to the younger ones: the % of older in 2050 will be even more important than today, in all countries, especially in Western ones.

The numbers were right, but the analysis deeply wrong: in 2050, the seniors will be the Millennials! One who is born a Millennials will die a Millennial and the set of values that one generation share, deeply, tend to remain at all ages. This is another reason why Millennials should drive our plans: if we learn to engage with them, if we design our brands and our communication with the purpose to speak to them, we will be prepared for our next consumers.

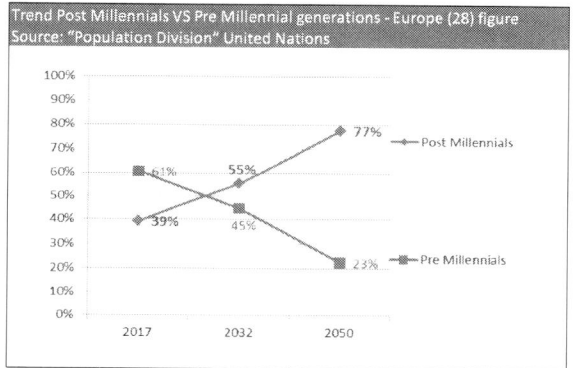

But that doesn't explain everything, which is also because in a lot of these economies two consumers out of every three are adults and seniors, and it will need a number of years before they disappear off the marketing screens.

The point here is a different one, Millennials are an influence group and a culture of reference for marketing: **Millennials are the most reasonable representation of the future** and that is why they are the culture of reference for marketing.

But before specifying the reasons for their influence, let us look more closely at some more figures to better understand the relationship between young people and the digital world.

Millennials and the digital world[16]

Millennials have grown up in the digital world, connected through every kind of device that technology has made available to them over the years, from early adolescence up to now. The more we move forward, the more all of us will live in a connected world and we will be grouped together with Millennials, but for the moment there is still not an insignificant watershed between young people and those who are not young, between those who know how to use technology and those who don't. Consequently there is a part of the population that can do some things digitally, and another part that can't. There is also a strong watershed between those who grew up with technology and those who have had to learn it. There is a different level of familiarity with digital objects between a Millennial and a greying executive, even though both use computers and smartphones every day with the same skills: what characterises these young people isn't so much the availability of Internet – which can be used from a computer, smartphone or in any other way possible from now on – but their natural capacity to use the Internet for different activities in daily life. **For Millennials, technology is transparent, and that is a basic difference.**

I am going to mention an anecdote that I also told in *#Generation 2.0* and left readers with a strong idea of the *Always on*[17] or *Never off* concept of these young people:

"There are two young fish who are swimming alongside one another when they find an older fish swimming in the opposite direction, who waves at them and says "Good morning boys. What's the water like today?". The two young fish continue swimming along for a bit, then one of them looks at the other and asks: "What the hell is water?".

---

[16] The figures in this section have been largely taken from research carried out by Kantar TNS for Google called "Consumer Barometer", which were redrawn by the author to analyse young people aged 15 to 34, resident in high-GDP countries (for other data and for methodological details: www.consumerbarometer.com)

[17] To raise a smile, enjoy these illustrations by Ajit Jhonson on the connected generation, thought up while he was taking a doctorate at the University of Edinburgh http://www.wired.it/internet/web/2015/04/03/generazione-always-on-progetto-illustrazioni/

If we want to understand Millennials, we thus have to go further than elements relating to web use and get involved in the motivations and ways in which they use it in everyday life: from what they do to how they behave, they look the same, but their behaviour and the issues that drive them are very different.

As has been mentioned several times, the scope of this analysis is not limited to attributing a special character to this generation just because they use the Internet: their specific characteristic, which really makes them a definable generation, is the fact that they have grown up in connected worlds and have shaped their way of being, their values, and their view of things and the future on this. So if we look carefully at behaviour, similarities can be found between a Millennial and a "digital immigrant", but it is only with the former group that technology has had an impact beyond behaviour and has actually shaped a generation, having had an impact on the individual and social self of young people, projecting it in a strengthened and "augmented" world".

Let's go back to the figures, the starting point for marketing: to fully understand the sense of change taking place, we should look carefully at some symptomatic behaviour.

1) *Millennials go on line every day.*

This is essentially not really a very surprising fact, but let us try and analyse it for what it says and in terms of its implications for marketing, starting with actually recognising that we should not (any longer) say of Millennials that they "go online" but more accurately that they "are online".

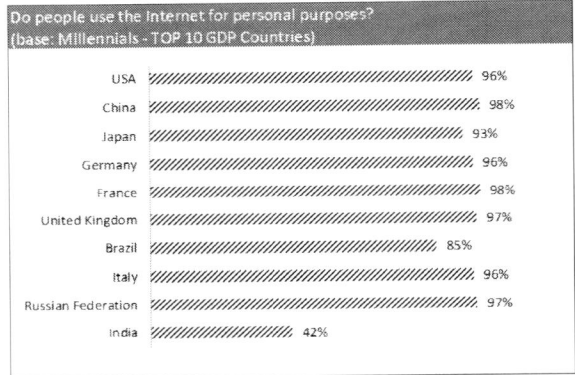

Do people use the Internet for personal purposes? (base: Millennials - TOP 10 GDP Countries)	
USA	96%
China	98%
Japan	93%
Germany	96%
France	98%
United Kingdom	97%
Brazil	85%
Italy	96%
Russian Federation	97%
India	42%

Millennials are connected, with several devices, and of these, almost all of them connect every day.

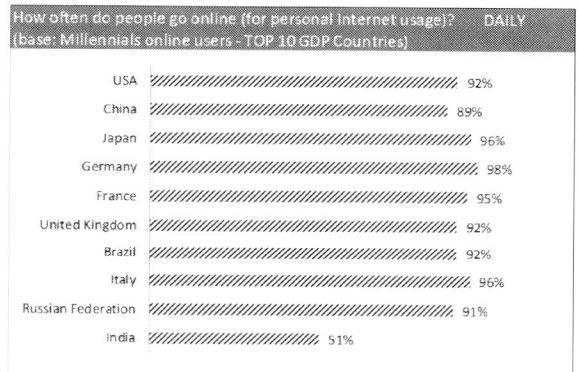

However it is precisely this fact that often leads to one of the most misleading interpretations which means looking at Millennials just in terms of their online life. Underlying that, there is perhaps a lot of the approach of those analysts who, simplistically, interpret things just through antithesis: those who watch television and those who don't watch it, those who consume and those who don't, those who see the product in one way, and those who don't. With a fact like this we should rather be led to consider, like the two fish we mentioned, that young people can continuously flow between on and offline. They use the web for a range of different reasons, from more game-based ones to more serious ones, for entertainment and for study, for work and to decide what to buy. But that doesn't mean that they only exist online, as is often said. They exist and that is that, on and offline, according to the given moment. The distinction between on and offline is more ours than theirs, and it is something to immediately give up if we want to embrace Post Millennial Marketing.

The base concept behind the Internet penetration figure is thus what ought to lead us to understanding the countless possibilities that one has to converse with and reach Millennials: forgetting about their so-called offline life or the use of other, non-digital communication media would be a serious mistake. That is also because, within a short time, even the media that are currently not, will become connected – from television to radio, right up to the press. **Looking at Millennials thus helps us to begin to deal with the future,** when all media will be connected and we will be able to flick through a hard-copy magazine (so without a supporting device), navigating between the links, watching videos of the pages and receiving geo-targeted advertising. Thinking that a target is always potentially online means we can think in a multi-channel way, and bring the focus onto the content of the communication and not the medium used.

2) *Millennials are great users of communication media.*

If we look more closely at the concept which is explained above, and break out the data using an analysis of the various kind of communication media used by Millennials, we will be able to get rid of any bias, however for or against digital things it is.

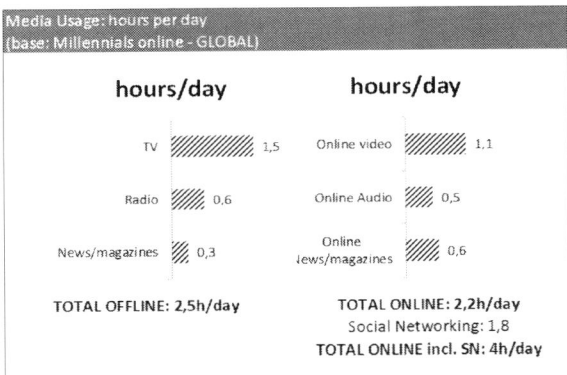

So if the use of various communication media is analysed, it can be seen that Millennials manage to have a much more articulated use than what a lot of us think: we who seek at all costs to restrict and stereotype them in a purely digital way[18].

What digital usage means for these young people is greater use of content, visuals, audio, news, magazines or whatever. The big suggestion (and teaching) that Millennials bring is thus to assess the new opportunities that we are supplied with by the very integration of different communication media, which thanks to the combined use of digital and analogical, is being implemented to a significant degree. The Millennials enjoy content, not communication media! If indeed we want to put a stop to the sterile "war" between off and online, which is still very typical of Marketing 1.0, we actually have to start from the figures which show equal use of the two kinds of communication media: offline (2,5 hours per day) and online media (2,2 hours per day, excluding the time spent on Social Networks) are equally sources which allow Millennials to use the contents mentioned above, even though the two have different approaches to production and usage.

3) *Millennials use a smartphone to go online.*

Another figure that won't surprise anybody is that for smartphone ownership, but what does it really mean? That is the question that we should ask ourselves as marketing people, if we want to understand the sense of change and prepare ourselves for emerging trends.

I would say that the name "mobile" is a bit misleading here: the term "mobile marketing" shows that the special feature of this technique lies in allowing consumers to be activated while mobile, but that isn't the issue. In this case too, we should let ourselves be helped by the figures, and we should analyse which behaviour is activated by going online using mobile devices.

---

[18] Source: "Connected Life" research conducted by Kantar TNS on around 1,000 connected consumers in countries which were the subject of the research (http://connectedlife.tnsglobal.com/)

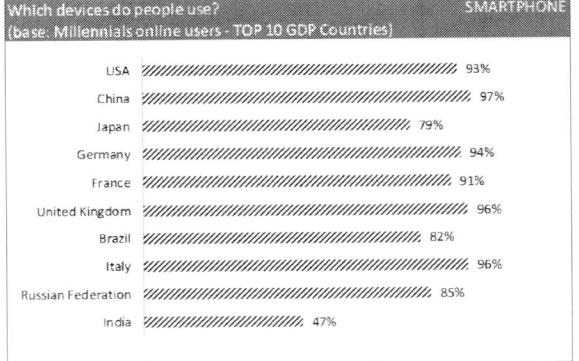

Let us concentrate our attention on some areas of behaviour that Generation X wasn't able to experience when young, since their cellphones at that time could only be used to make calls and send text messages.

For what daily life activities do people use their smartphone? (base: Millennials online users - TOP 10 GDP Countries)	Listen to music	Play games	Take photos/videos
USA	54%	46%	65%
China	69%	55%	76%
Japan	37%	43%	56%
Germany	44%	44%	56%
France	41%	41%	58%
United Kingdom	47%	34%	55%
Brazil	66%	43%	66%
Italy	40%	41%	64%
Russian Federation	59%	36%	63%
India	80%	70%	67%

These activities, which amongst other things represent new opportunities to activate marketing which are already available, make us understand that connectivity by mobile phone isn't just connectivity on the move. A smartphone is a communication device, not a turbo-powered mobile phone, or a computer with a reduced size screen! It means we can talk and listen, read and play, to save and to send, to get information and to post, both away from and at home.

We can say that connectivity through mobile systems has an impact on the way that media is consumed, from at least three important points of view. Usage of communication media is:

a) more and more individual
b) joined together with other communication media
c) interactive, in every occasion, given use of the Internet on the move

It is now clear that marketing engagement connected to the three implications cited above can go well beyond advertising on smartphones. They talk of one-to-one marketing, opportunities for cross-media storytelling, integration with events and meeting moments with the brand, both physical and virtual, if we want to still use that terminology for it.

The effect of this on television usage is significant:

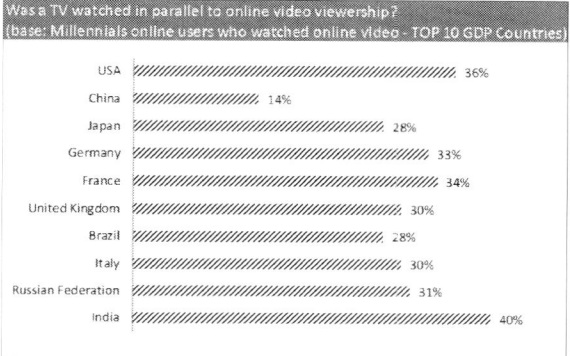

One in three Millennials has watched a video online over the past week, and has done so while they watched television. The implications of this way of using communication media is devastating from several points of view. Just think of television viewing figures during advertising breaks: Millennials no longer change channels when advertising comes on, instead their eyes and fingers turn to their smartphones. There is no trace of this in television viewing surveys, which assess channel audiences and that direct billions of spending from media centres: with no zapping taking place, the viewing figures for a given advertising break stay the same, even though people's attention is directed elsewhere.

If we look at these phenomena from other points of view, however, smartphones bring an enormous increase in opportunities for marketing people, if they break free from the mindset of having to choose and instead work on integrating on and offline.

New technologies offer more opportunities than risks
(base: Millennials online users - TOP 10 GDP Countries)

Country	%
USA	44%
China	64%
Japan	44%
Germany	42%
France	37%
United Kingdom	62%
Brazil	57%
Italy	46%
Russian Federation	57%
India	79%

4) *Millennials make comparisons to make a decision.*

Only one out of ten Millennials heard of a product for the first time from advertising.

From this analysis we learn how damaging it is to consider Millennials as an audience and not as a generation characterised by their own rules and behaviour. A product is bought by Millennials after they have talked about it with other people, both on and offline, both with friends and with strangers: it is an attitude, which is actually formed in adolescence, that Millennials take with them in normal, everyday life, without having even the awareness of deploying it.

Another warning that this analysis offers us is respect for and the importance of a brand. Let's take the Italian figure as an example: the same number of Millennials say they have obtained information on a new product in conversations between "peers", on and offline, as from the brand itself. A good previous experience with a brand is the best channel of access to the product. Advertising is not enough, however, to build a brand with Millennials (let's say it once again, whether on or offline!): only 10% of Millennials say they heard of a product for the first time from advertising. We return again to the heart of the argument and ask ourselves what is the real reason underlying this result.

Imagine a young person who learns how to choose, assess, make his own ideas and give his own opinions on forums, blogs and social networks where there are countless options and multiple viewpoints: the attitude that he will have developed is to continually check his theories and opinions from the start. If we now apply this mindset to the world of marketing, we can understand how just advertising is no longer able to influence buying behaviour: this will have to be validated or enriched by opinions coming from as many sources as possible.

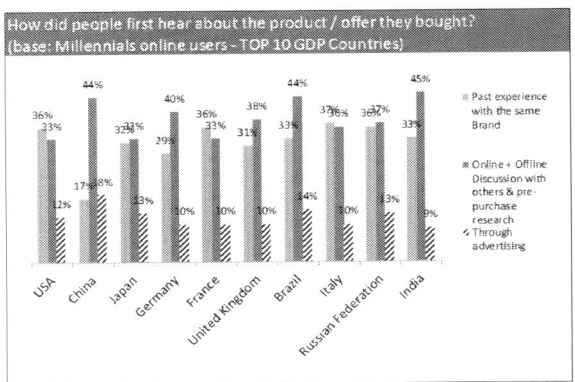

A brand that doesn't consider this fundamental aspect in the way that Millennials reach a decision will spend too much on advertising: not because the campaign isn't correct from a technical point of view, but because the social dynamic in which the campaign will operate has not been considered. Advertising is just one of a number of elements to influence purchases and, most of all, users will extract from this the most interesting and useful elements to share opinions with other people: advertising must intrinsically contain word-of-mouth elements.

5) *Millennials live the context and the moment.*

Millennials have grown up with a different concept of time: something on the Internet can be both short-lived and ever-lasting at the same time. Imagine growing up following content that disappears after a moment or which comes to light again on your Facebook page after years, following a few too many "likes". The mental category of time, with which we perceive the things around us, takes on a very different meaning from the past: it doesn't spell out the passing of events in a linear way, from a "before" to an "after", giving them a rating and a significance.

A post made two years ago on TripAdvisor influences us as if it were written today, something that happened years ago comes back to the present day if it becomes relevant in social media, my reputation is based on what I am like now, but even more so on what I have been like. On the other hand, it is as if the future doesn't exist: the uncertainty of the social and economic situation, together with the Millennials' natural attitude to living for the moment, destroys any wish to predict, to protect, to think in the long term. If you talk with a Millennial, don't ask them what they want to do when they grow up, or how they see themselves in five years' time, because they won't know what to say. But this is not through ignorance: it is through an inability and lack of interest in looking too far ahead. They know that everything changes, sometimes instantly, they know that the most important thing is what happens today, they know that nothing is certain about the future. Imagine yourself having grown up in a world in which a promotional banner disappears for ever if you don't click on it immediately, or in which your childhood friends return after years and years of silence, and you then find out that they are basically the same as they were before. Essentially, as far as the Millennial Mindset is concerned, time doesn't flow, and disappears from experience.

Nowadays all of us have to experience time in this way. That is the world of today. But the Millennials have grown up in it, this environment has shaped them, and has shaped them structurally, with consequences on their way of being and experiencing situations.

A Millennial lives the here and now, participating in the context and what is happening, giving weight to specific moments and makes vertical incursions into what he or she interprets as real events, which are to be followed and built with the community.

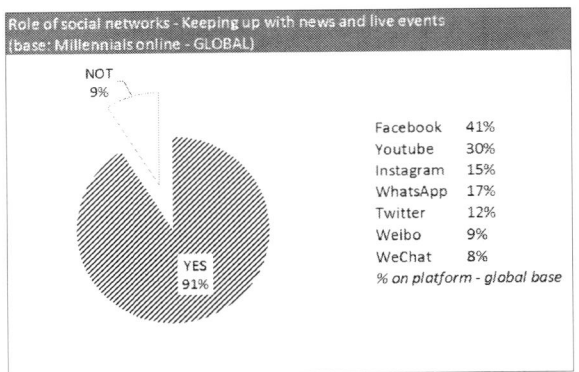

This natural attitude from the Millennials teaches us a lot: it teaches us to support our children at times in which they don't plan for the future but rather live their own lives, it teaches us to manage Millennial employees, who don't seem very interested in professional development and long-term career paths. It teaches us how to do marketing: the way of doing marketing today – which has been developed over the past fifty years on theories about communication and consumers – is not relevant for Millennials. You have to be careful, it hasn't lost all relevance because this or that product is no longer in fashion, or because they consume in a different way, or because they don't watch television any more.

Marketing has lost relevance because it doesn't take account of the context, of topicality, or of the present. Marketing is still thinking with decision-making processes that last for weeks, and of sequential communication dynamics. It still thinks that you just have to be Top of Mind to be able to get back in someone's mind when a purchase is being made, and it still thinks that a brand should be for ever. Post Millennial Marketing changes this outlook: it starts from what is happening today to build itself a history and a meaning, not vice-versa. A good communicator nowadays thinks and moves as a good journalist would do: he or she knows how to grasp what is trending and rides the news, providing distinctive storytelling and their own interpretation.

A brand must become an opinion leader that knows how to live the context, that acts in response to occurrences that are relevant to the consumer.

6) *Millennials ask for value.*

Millennial behaviour that is definitely difficult to put up with is their attempting in every possible way to avoid advertising. They skip pre-rolls on YouTube, they use their smartphones when television advertising comes on, they activate Ad Blocking systems: at the time of writing, thirty per cent of Italian Millennials are estimated to have installed Ad Blocking.

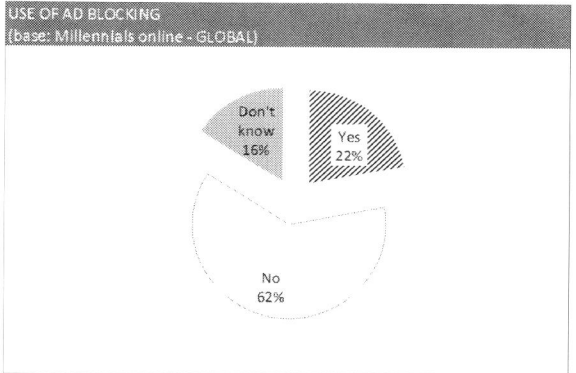

Marketing people find them really intolerable! Of course, for people who have been used to being able to interrupt the usage of a piece of content with television advertising, it has to be absolutely detestable having to put up with this affront. And yet, marketing has never been able to count on an army of such generous "viralisers" as it can now: young people are the source of success of the most successful campaigns, those which –

having pressed the right levers – win visibility free of charge through sharing on social networks.

It is not actually just a case of the Millennials taking up a position, as perhaps happened in the past. People liked advertising, appreciated it: the advertising that my grandmother watched was an art form, with advertising posters still displayed in exhibitions on the 20th century; what my mother watched was a short film sponsored by a brand; what I watched was an emotional display of my favourite product.

Or we hated it, when for example it interrupted the film that we were watching. Advertising was a kind of very specific content that interrupted the main content that people were looking at, in a magazine or on television, according to a clear and shared transactional set-up: a good film requires resources, you have to pay for resources with a tax, the cost of subscribing to SKY or by watching advertising. Advertising was necessary, and as such it was respected to an extent, even when it wasn't of interest.

Millennials have got a different mindset: they download films and watch television series before they even come out in our country, they don't pay for contents because the most amusing ones are often produced by other users, they have the online, free version of every newspaper and television channel, and access a huge range of contents on demand, and enjoy it in every place and on various different occasions.

Most of all, when advertising comes on while they are watching a television programme, they don't get irritated, since it just gives them a chance to have a quick look at Facebook. For Millennials, advertising is not a matter of exchange, but of content that, to be enjoyed, needs to be informative or entertaining. Advertising people now more than ever have to fish for attention, and cannot count on the audience being ready to watch. Advertising is no longer automatically part of the game, it has to have a role.

That issue brings our attention to a fundamental aspect of how brand content is used: relevance. Millennials have grown up with the idea of having an infinite amount of informational resources from which to choose, and that is why their approach is much more active than what it was in the past. A Millennial has a natural approach to research, selection and assessment of pieces of information that he or she has in front of them in using contents, because that is the imprinting they have taken from using the web. If a brand takes the first steps, moving forward without having been sought out, then it will have to be extremely relevant, at that time and for that person because the alternative on a smartphone can always be activated. Millennials can and must choose between the infinite possibilities that they have in front of their eyes and in their hands, and not just use it passively.

Generation X's approach to advertising is actually different to that of Millennials: the former have a usage mindset, whereas the second have an assessment approach; for the former group it is an established fact, but for the latter it is an option; for the former it is a price to be paid, for the latter it is content to be used, at some stage.

That is the reason why either advertising should be extraordinarily appealing from a creative point of view, or it is best to use other communication media to inform, to provide service, to give discounts, or any value in exchange, provided it is recognised.

7) *Millennials give value.*

The debate on the relevance of Millennials for companies hasn't yet finished. Beyond the cases in which the penetration of young people amongst consumers of a brand and specific products is significant (amongst other things because of the very numerous goods categories, from beverages to travel), there is not yet any convergence as to their value: some people feel they are too few, if compared with the entire population (indeed, being a segment it couldn't be otherwise); for others they are penniless and don't have any buying power, and are often still living at home with their parents; for others they are too difficult, incoherent or incomprehensible. For others, Millennials have become a real obsession: everyone is talking about them, the bosses want them, they are the secret of success in the most viral campaigns and the ones that win the most awards.

If we look beyond the positions that have been taken, we must again let the figures decide rather than our inclinations and stereotypes. There is one reason above all why we have to keep Millennials in marketing strategies and projects: Millennials influence the choices of various parts of the population in many kinds of purchases.

Their decision was made through processes of social assessment, which makes them an extraordinary source of word-of-mouth and viral communication flows, which impact on other consumers, who will have looked for that information, or will have been subjected to it without their asking for it. But be careful, this is not a reference just to the dynamics existing in social networks: the Millennials' cognitive process, both through the digital world and in so-called real life, moves through continual checks, research and answers. They have grown up like this, they haven't learnt it later: they don't think that a shop assistant is the only and most expert point of reference when making a purchase, and the same is also true of their relationships with their parents, when life is involved.

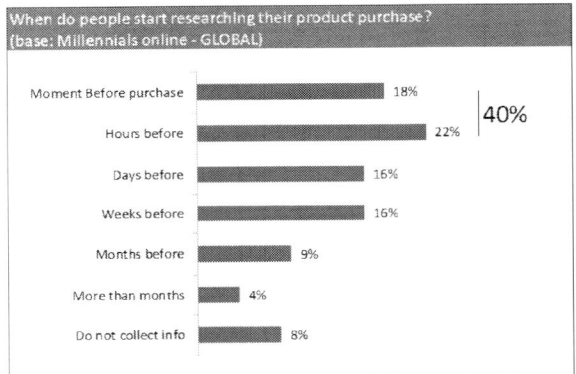

That is their natural approach when they take decisions: they are no longer just passively receiving, but are always interactive and communicative; that is the phenomenon that creates the spread of opinions and the consequent – powerful – word of mouth, both on and offline. They are influenced by nature, but not because somebody has authorised them to be so, with certificates, prizes or followers.

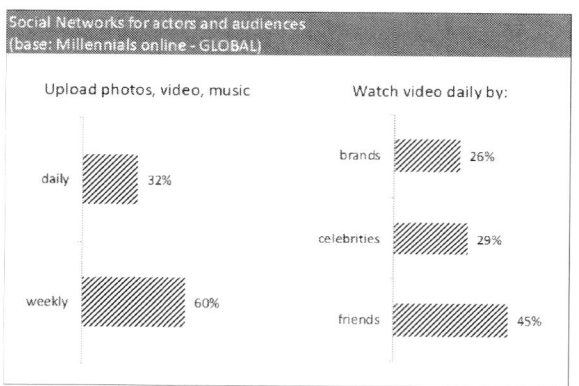

Furthermore, and no less important: Millennials are tremendously attracted by new things and so are the number one target to be reached in a product launch, and the ones that will determine the success or failure of an innovative product. Targeting and pleasing Millennials, in different areas and product types, not just in a technological environment, is crucial for the success of a product, since from them comes a large part of the innovation and its "validation" by other consumers, however young or old they may be.

Millennials should thus interest all marketing people, beyond their relevance as consumer targets, because:

- They are the most active and prolific source of influence
- They are the first to take on, assess and spread the news of an innovation or a marketing development
- They are great communicators, from whom we can learn

Millennials and myths to be dismantled (with figures)

In recent years people have talked a lot about Millennials and a lot more will be written soon. But too often young people are described in a stereotyped way, with few supporting details and with views distorted by personal beliefs or experiences: Millennials storytelling is often made of (negative) myths.

1) Narcissists.

They are constantly posting what they are doing, who they are with, where they are, what they are trying, taking photos and uploading videos which are often surreal. And then there are *Instagrammers*, *YouTubers*, *Bloggers*, *Selfie-maniacs* ... but watch out, they are not personalities that are dependent on narcissist gestures[19].

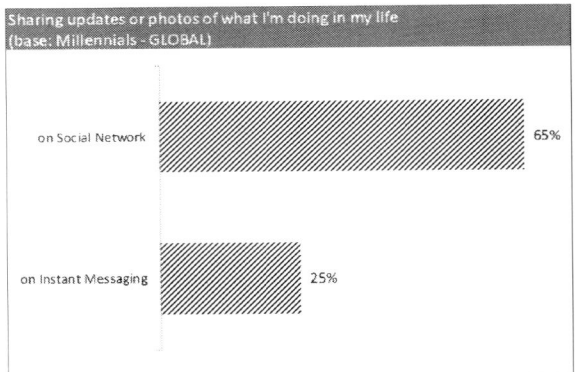

---

[19] www.telegraph.co.uk/women/womens-life/11265022/Selfie-obsession-are-we-the-most-narcissistic-generation-ever.html

For Millennials, sharing experiences (never simple information, even those that appear to be such) is a fundamental prerogative of their social being, not a choice of self-complacency. It isn't saying "Hi, I'm here, who can see me?", but a simple expression of presence, often done to share and provoke a response in a co-creational way. A selfie is a perfect gesture of communication, which can put over in a single stroke who the subject of the photo is, the moment, what the feeling is. Companies can learn a lot from Millennials if they want to find out how to communicate a grouping so full of elements in an instantaneous way: if we really looked at the way Millennials communicate, their attention to "likes" and answers to their audience, the care they take in picking filters and views, their innate capacity to be in the moment and of giving their personal, light but authentic interpretation of what is happening now, the attention with which they tag, involve, and get their peers involved...

Perhaps it is a new communication technique, in marketing, and we could call it *"brand selfism"*: a brand often puts itself over in a very basic way (the product) or a very pretentious way (the brand), other times it puts over its consumers' lifestyle and their needs, other times the place in which it can be found... brand selfism could be the way in which a brand puts itself over to create empathy with its consumers, starting from the experience had from the brand itself in a given context and with given consumers, becoming human and personal, just like the users with which it is talking.

An impractical suggestion in a simple way, but definitely a suggestion which could be worth looking into further[20]: the practice of taking selfies doesn't just talk of a way of communicating, it talks of new ways of relating with others (with consumers?) and an expression of themselves (of the brand?) which is much wider, and studied by lots of people from a psychological, social and cultural viewpoint. Have a look here: www.selfieresearchers.com

---

[20] A similar concept of Brand Selfism is mentioned as a technique to create communications that are truly attractive and interactive :
www.adweek.com/digital/shaul-olmert-playbuzz-guest-post-content-for-the-selfie-generation/

2) **Xenophiles.**

When it comes to under developed countries, from an economic or from a political perspective, too often media talk about brain drains, with young people judged to see the world outside as being more aspirational compared with the country of origin: in reality, leaving behind those countries with huge political issues, the percentage of migrants amongst Millennials is less than in the past. Furthermore, if you ask young people what company they would like to work for, alongside the tech cult brands (Google, Microsoft, etc) they will mention successful local big companies which have nevertheless been able to win themselves an international standing, like for example Ferrari, FCA, Barilla, Ferrero are for younger Italians[21].

Geographical position does not, therefore, influence the preferences of these young people. On the contrary, Italian things are better if a choice is available, provided that it does not mean being restricted to local things, in every sense, from office relocation to management style. Space, as we knew it, doesn't any longer exist for Millennials, who are used to travelling with just a few euros, and are connected with the whole world with just a click, and who are used to reading and answering posts in various languages, even helped by Google Translator. That is good news for Italian companies, but also for multinationals that are no longer associated with a distant and far-off world.

3) **Inert and pessimistic about the future.**
To us they seem to lack bite, energy and the will to fight, as if they were happy whatever happens. And yet they are the most interactive and informed generation in history: thanks to the web, they have absorbed much more information than entire generations would have heard in the past.

It's true, they haven't got plans for the future, and if you ask them to think about what they are going to do when they grow up, they will reply uncertainly, but that is not a reason for us to judge them with our own eyes, those of people who were born with outlooks that were definite or taken as such. Millennials don't have such a broad horizon, they consider projects and not long-term programmes, but that doesn't make them pessimistic and

---

[21] http://www.linkiesta.it/it/article/2014/10/02/i-ragazzi-vogliono-la-meritocrazia-non-il-posto-fisso/23022/

incapable of participating in their own future. They give themselves or ask for a short-term goal, and commit themselves to it. For the same reason, they tend not to be faithful to brands: from time to time they pick the brand that works best for their project: don't ask them to take part in loyalty programmes, but seek to achieve relevance to their goals at all times.

4) **Compulsive and frivolous buyers.**

They don't look after their money, they instantly fall in love with and then buy the stupidest things that they may find in front of them. We see them using computers or cellphones and responding in a frenetic way to stimuli without reflecting. Are we certain of this? Having grown up with the Internet means having acquired an approach to the decision-making process which is much more ponderous and rational than in the past. Every decision to buy is preceded by checking on social media, and even at the very moment when they enter a shop they can count on this, their own "personal shopper", by using a cellphone to look for the characteristics and best prices for a product that a shop assistant has just handed to them.

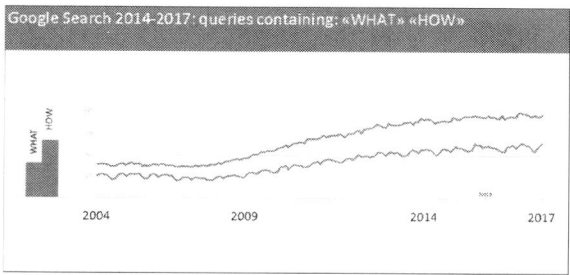

It is true, they are attracted by surprising communication and that is why they are tremendously attached to brands. But now the effect of the other three Ps[22] (product, price, placement) on young people today is still more important than promotion: the product must have top quality features,

---

[22] A reference to Kotler's 4P model, mentioned earlier.

which are confirmed by the community, the price and distribution have to ensure accessibility and a "fast track" to the desired brand.

5) **They don't read any more.** Millennials read more than seniors and they read much more than what current elders did in the past, when they were younger. No past generation has ever read so much, or has been as curious and thirsty for information that can easily be found online on websites, blogs, forums and social networks. They have grown up with a reading mindset, and they can't do without it: their approach to looking for information, comparison and surfing data is a basic quality that identifies the new rules of relationship with the surrounding world. Whether it is on tweets, websites, a Wikipedia article or a long thread on a forum, they read to get information before, during and after the moment of product consumption. They also read a lot of newspapers, magazines, books... even though they are not necessarily those that have been printed and bought in a bookshop: newspapers are much more widely read by this generation, if we consider all devices that could be used to access the text. So they read: books, newspapers, posts... but also product labels, company information, etc. The act of trying to inform oneself is the product of their personal attitude, which was born in the web world and is Google-centric.

On the other hand, their way of communicating and the expectations they have from brands are more and more visual, icon-related and cinematographic so as to win impact and attention. How do we reconcile the need for information from this generation with the need for entertaining, visual and immediate communication?

For now, by avoiding choosing a single medium and a single means of communication to talk about the brand: noting changes of opinion online is no longer enough, you have to enter and play a role, in User Generated areas or in one's own official social media environment. Facebook page, Twitter profile, YouTube, LinkedIn, Instagram... but also a suitable website and one for mobile devices, which can comprehensively answer right along the consumer's decision-making path. They are essential touch points to make demanding Millennials read and use the brand, using immediate and engaging communication styles.

6) **Not faithful to a brand.**

This is actually true, but seen in a way that is different from what we might imagine. There are indeed a large number of brands that can win their trust, and which can conquer them as consumers and keep them over time. Top of the list is Apple, a brand which was born for this generation and thanks to which has grown amongst all the other population groups. They are brands which respect the rules of relationship between Millennials and by which Millennials measure companies, from a product point of view, but also in terms of communication and social behaviour.

These are companies that have been able to insert themselves into the conversation with young people with the right S.T.Y.L.E, putting forward relevant arguments and their own role; companies that have always behaved transparently, which are authentic and open to feedback; which have been able to anticipate the sudden moves in the market and quickly reply with product solutions and up-to-date marketing moves; accessible brands – albeit ones that are sometimes expensive – that have allowed mobile behaviour, personalised relationship paths, and dynamism; they are brands that have focused everything on customer experience at every touch point.

These are the characteristics that make a brand successful with Millennials[23]. But let's not talk about loyalty: Millennials can put their relationship with their brand to the test a million times a day. They are the generation of ratings, stars and "likes"! So you can't talk about loyalty in a strict sense, but – when it happens – rather of long-term relationships which are won at all times and in every area.

7) **Online shopping only**.

There are reasons why they prefer online purchases and avidly avoid going to a physical point of sale. Obviously the lack of accessibility of a point of sale is one of the reasons why they will go to e-commerce channels, for example if the product can only be found in the UK, and so on. But if we look beyond objective impediments, there are reasons and specific situations in which Millennials love e-commerce.

Making a purchase after having received a good piece of advice is the most natural thing you can do: e-commerce platforms reduce the anxiety prior to purchase and mean that a wish can be turned into a product.

Another reason why young people prefer e-commerce is the possibility of choosing between products: Millennials appreciate, and even say they

---

[23] These are elements of the S.T.Y.L.E. that we will deal with at greater length further on.

see as necessary, a breadth of choice. In the same way, opening hours will never be flexible enough compared to the web.

There are other elements, however, which mean that Millennials prefer buying in a point of sale. Of these the most important is in the customer experience sphere: the act of purchase is a moment of gratification and entertainment for young people, and that is why the most successful stores with this demographic group are precisely those in which the buying experience and product try-out is just one – and perhaps the last – of a series of moments of relating with the brand, with its values, with the stories it has to tell which can be presented at the point of sale. So if you see the online part of your product's sales growing, to the detriment of offline sales, without having done anything to encourage this... ask yourself if your product isn't becoming a commodity for this target group and isn't offering any other experience occasion with which to connect with consumers.

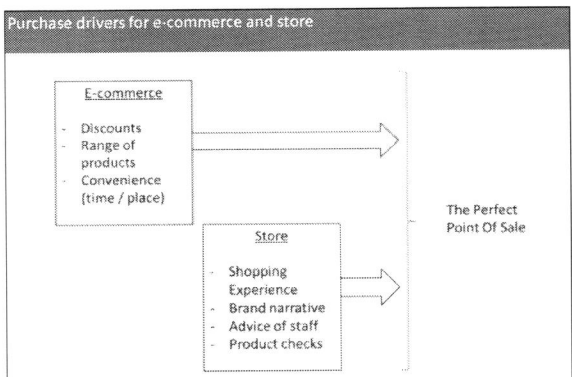

For Millennials (as for the fish and water), there is no reason why there should be differences in the fundamental aspects of customer experience and in expected benefits between a physical and a virtual store.

8) **The brand no longer matters**, a friend is better.

Millennials say "friends and family" are influencing sources on their purchase decisions, and put the point of sale in second place, while less youngers give this role to the brand website and much more less to advertising . By contrast, for every other generation it is the point of sale which is the main source of influence, even for more digital segments: the store has always been the place where the idea of buying meets the product, and the latest information which is useful in making the decision, such as price, pack and promotional material. But what is happening with these kids? Do you really just need the opinion of a friend to render worthless millions of euros in advertising budget, years of product research and development, and perhaps a lengthy history and millions of servings all around the world?

But that is how it is. Google calls it ZMOT ("Zero Moment Of Truth", https://www.thinkwithgoogle.com/collections/zero-moment-truth.html).
The moment of truth with a product which precedes the purchase at a point of sale (first moment) and consumption (second moment). It is the time between thinking of a purchase and defining the solution, often spent on opinion and review websites, social networks and websites to understand what the best choice would be. That isn't the case for all product categories, of course: there are routine or basic purchases for which purchases don't proceed in this way; but for many other purchases this actually is the process. Indeed Millennials no longer say, once they have decided to buy a product "well, let's go to the shop and have a look", but instead "Let's have a quick Google of it and then we can go to the shop and see if it's worth it". Has the "shop" factor been substituted by the Internet? You really have to see things in a sequential rather than a substitutional way: friends, or the web in general, can't substitute the value created around a brand by marketing stimuli, but instead integrate with them. That is why people say that brands are no longer important for young people today. A brand, or the grouping of values that marketing and communication can generate around a product, is still extremely relevant, of course. But we have to remember that these values are nowadays being continually checked by Millennials, through experiences told by others, friends or otherwise, found on and offline.

However, what does essentially change in comparison with previous generations, is the way of bringing out the brand's features. For Millennials, a brand is strong if it manages to create an emotional connection based on the concept of similarity, and no longer that of aspiration. Brands most linked to young people are not brands that show an ideal world to which to aspire, but brands which one can feel similar to, because of what they show, what they are, and what they do. This is the concept of "brand bonding" for young people today: closeness, recognisability, feeling part of the same way of doing and thinking. But if we think of a brand as if it were the star of a heroic film, then we can only agree with those consultants who say that a brand no longer means anything today for young people. The error is probably right there: the brand is an element of great attraction for young people, but the reasons for affection and engagement have changed from what they were in the past. Brand Trust is a more important factor than Brand Awareness, recognised value is greater than the value of recognition.

9) You just have to keep them amused.

A fundamental element to have a relationship with Millennials is their wish to be constantly entertained. This view says that the various times of contact with the brand, from the decision to buy to the moment of consumption up to post-sales, should be entertaining moments: not a "touch point" but an "experience point", we could say. So yes, if an initiative – whether it be a piece of advertising or a post on Facebook – is fun, it will have a greater chance of attracting attention, drawing approval and being circulated on social media, because irony and a laugh are the emotional stimuli that engage. That, however, doesn't mean that it is just being entertained that moves "likes" and "shares": every initiative that is able to incite emotional engagement will have the same chance of success, whether it is a parody or an emotional story.

In this case too, then, we have to be careful of simplifications and prejudices: Millennials love to have fun, clearly, like all young people throughout history, sometimes in a carefree way; but what sets them apart from other young generations from the past, is their constant search for emotions, experiences and immersion in things. Having grown up with social media has meant acquiring this necessity to always experience things at first hand, in an interactive and participatory way, and to share these experiences with other people. It is thus not enough to entertain them, even though that is an effective means of attracting them: if anything it is enough (so to say…) to develop engaging initiatives, whether fun or not, and with these encourage users in an immersive way. The role of creativity is thus fundamental, but for Millennials this is missing something important, it has no mechanisms of engagement which are capable of stimulating the user's experience and immersion. Interaction, gamification, role-playing, virtuality, etc are some of the techniques which can be used in this approach. Perhaps that is why Silicon Valley companies ask engineers to take part in creative meetings.

The creative work of an advertising person should be a stimulus to the creativity of young people, that's probably the trick: is that a step backwards for advertising people? No, rather it is very probably a great step forward towards Millennials! Being creative in the ways in which consumers are engaged and made creative is, beyond the content of the message, a necessity which cannot be dispensed with: it is no longer a media planning issue that advertising agencies can avoid.

10) **They no longer watch television.**

There are no firm statistics proving that the viewing of television content amongst young people has decreased much more than it did with adult generations: some of the usage dynamics and those involving shifts between media are a market trend amongst all segments of the connected population. Indeed, if it is true that so-called traditional media are tending to lose audiences to digital media to some extent amongst all targets, since there are greater entertainment content usage opportunities with other devices, it is also true that – if we add together the "many TVs" that we must nowadays take account of (television content put on websites by the broadcaster, or which can be seen on YouTube itself) - viewing amongst young people would turn out to be greater than it once was. What counts is therefore not analysing media from the point of view of the device, if we want to follow how Millennials think: what actually matters is content, not the way in which it is broadcast. That is why there are successful television programmes - including ones that are successful amongst young people – and programmes which lose audience, regardless of the digital strategies that they deploy.

Thus: if young people don't watch television, it isn't so much because they find it old or because they don't find it an engaging way of viewing content, but because they are used to being at the centre of interaction and activities carried on with multiple devices they have at hand. So if anything it is the content that is not engaging, regardless of the author's idea of spreading a hashtag with which to tweet. Involvement, interaction, and immersion in the television programme thus depends mainly on the content and the shape it has been given: it will be the Millennials to make it circulate on the various digital platforms, if they think it is interesting. Let us no longer ask, then, if television is still an appropriate medium for young people, but rather whether the content is really in line with Millennials. Look at the viewing figures of programmes like X Factor, their profile and the level of engagement created. Then, if you want, you can even compare it with other musical programmes, but don't confuse medium and content.

Chapter IV – THE S.T.Y.L.E. OF MILLENNIALS

Millennial-consumers: needs and values[24]

Millennials have acquired a "web mindset" from when they were adolescents: they have grown up with the idea that everything can be got quickly, that information is always available, that there is no one who you can't get in touch with and that you can do so at any moment; they have understood that they can make a successful video even without being a director, that they can rate a product without being experts, that they can comment on advertising with its originators without themselves being creatives, that they can write a blog and talk to tens of thousands of users, without being a celebrity.

They have grown up and become adults in this way and now they no longer know how to work out if these dynamics are only possible on the web or also "outside". The truth is that young people don't even ask themselves this question.

Because of this, you often find that they are intolerant in shops, for example: compared to their expectations, the warehouse will always be too small, the products too common, the assistant not knowledgeable enough, with the owner not very much inclined to change the offer to fit in with something they suggest, and so on.

They grew up on the Web 2.0 and now transpose into the so-called real world, without further elaboration, all the values and dynamics existing in the collaborative environment of the web. That is what characterises them: a **"Millennial Mindset"** which acts on their way of behaving, of talking and thinking. They have their own style, which was born on the web but is then experienced in every aspect of life. Indeed, they have a "S.T.Y.L.E" style: the combination of five base elements that makes up their way of seeing the world and acting.

---

[24] This chapter takes the base concept of S.T.I.L.E. which was spelled out in "#Generazione 2.0" by F. Capeci, *op.cit.*, drawing on the chapter entitled "Lo S.T.I.L.E. della Generazione 2.0" *(The STILE of Generation 2.0)*, with modifications.

What are these elements?

- **S** – **Sociability**: the desire for sharing, collaboration and networking;
- **T** – **Transparency**: the search for exchanging information between parties, loyalty, authenticity, dialogue, possibilities of reciprocal assessment;
- **Y** – **Yes, now**: the attitude of working with speed, reactivity, making the context fleeting and adopting a here-and-now view;
- **L** – **Liberty**: the attraction of being able to choose, of variety, of the accessibility of things, content, services, of products which don't even have a price (from the sharing economy to piracy), and of the chance to escape;
- **E** – **Experience**: the gratification sought and tried by the possibilities of playing, of receiving entertainment, customisation and immersion.

We can look more closely at each point: to understand Generation Y, we will have to get to know the "style" of their behaviour; to have a dialogue we will have to consider the "style" of our arguments.

S.ociability

Keywords: **#share #social #together #cocreation #buzz #trigger #call**

Never has a generation of young people communicated with their peers as much as the Millennials.

Young people from Generation X and previous generations had many limits: seeing one's friends at home created embarrassment, the fixed line phone couldn't be busy for too long, writing letters took time and dedication, talking on a mobile phone about this and that, or even sending text messages, ended up costing a lot.

But Millennials are by contrast always connected to their network of friends, alternately using their voice and their fingers, and are attached to WiFi coverage available on the street so as to be "always on" everywhere. They are always up to date and in contact with their group of friends, thanks to Facebook or Snapchat, with WhatsApp they can communicate instantly, and even when they listen to music – apparently on their own – they look for connections to other people, in choosing the playlist and sharing what they are listening to, as happens with Spotify: if an app doesn't enable them to connect with other users or with their social media profile, it loses some of its appeal.

They are constantly communicating, with text, pictures, videos, "likes" or shares, without any kind of restriction or control. A lot of their communication with others, moreover, aren't even intentional: it is the web that is registering and reproducing the actions done on Social Media, which again proposes and socialises people's activities. Growing up in this world has lowered Millennials' threshold of confidentiality and has increased their wish of always being there and of winning presence with respect to others. Freed by being on the web from kinds of conditioning which are typical of physical relationships, such as distance, time, or mutual understanding, this generation is now able to establish relationships with unprecedented ease. They have worked out how to communicate by replying to a post published some time earlier, and reactivate the conversation on their own network; they know how to ask for information from a user on the other side of the world, translating the language with Google Translator only in the most difficult cases; they know how to post their video or a photo and see the number of views grow in real time. With this generation the number of moments of communication with friends increases, but what increases further are the opportunities for communication with other people – whether or not they have met them in real life – who have the same interests, passions or requirements. Rather we could say that it is the very act of communication itself which creates the link, not the other way round: interaction on social networks, whether with a comment, a link or just a "like", immediately becomes visible to all one's own network, elevating an individual gesture to a socialised act.

Socialising in digital domains changes the approach of these young people in relation to every single experience, however on or offline. What adults could interpret as insolence, or their ability to establish a relationship and converse with absolutely anybody (even brands!), should be interpreted in a way that is completely new compared to the past: it is the awareness of being able to say something interesting to anybody, and to assume that they are nevertheless interested in listening.

One of the first things that needs to be understood if you want to establish a relationship with Millennials is thus the fact that you can't just do advertising with them, so you can't just think of spreading a message and wait for the results in the supermarket: Generation Y has got its ears, mouths and fingers connected, and they move in synch when they react to a communicative stimulus. They live with the idea that every act is – should be – intrinsically social, whether that is something that they want or that happens to them.

Furthermore, Millennials' communication are often aimed at pooling an experience, at giving an opinion, at sharing a personal, subjective viewpoint: they don't give (and don't look for) absolute and objective truths, but instead make their own subjective vision available, the one that comes from their own experience. This is another fundamental aspect for companies that want to communicate with them: listening to the experiences of individuals is essential, as is putting over the most emotional aspect of the brand and looking for a connection with the most intimate part of the consumer.

Generation X chose a product because it was a well-known brand, because of the image built up amongst their network of peers, because of the advertising messages received and the advice of the shop assistant:

Generation X made a choice after having drawn up this "objective" information, which is the same for all consumers. Whereas members of Generation Y back up these sources with a flood of individual experiences that they find online, looking for those that mean most to them, the experiences that they hope to have, or not have, once the purchase is completed: opinions go alongside information, subjectivity alongside objectivity, and there is a plurality of voices rather than just one.

That is why every proposal aimed at this generation must necessarily contain elements of social relationships: communication must be open and should encourage socialisation. It has to give networking opportunities, it has to become something different, precisely because of the work that the community will do on what is considered unfinished work, which is to be modified and developed. Television advertising in Post Millennial Marketing is aimed at generating discussion, to be a pretext for socialisation and seeks to cause or facilitate word of mouth; it doesn't set itself the sole goal of capturing the attention of consumers sitting on a sofa, hoping that they will then remember the brand at the time of purchase.

Generation Y socialises its thoughts and gestures for a number of reasons: to create communal knowledge and to give everybody the chance of starting from a more advanced position, to help and ask for help, to share joy and express pain. This kind of "socialising" says a lot about these young people. It says, for example, that their carefree sharing with anybody is not an act of superficiality, but an intrinsic characteristic of their way of experiencing things.

A communicator who has S.T.Y.L.E. thus gives up the kind of advertising communication which is aimed at an individual and his or her aspirations. Instead they look to communicate in an appetising way for socialisation, picking issues, formats, suitable vehicles for what the consumer will do before, during and after a purchase, within their community.

T.ransparency

Keywords: **#trust #real #dialogue #evaluation #peer #nofrills**

For this generation, talking about what has been experienced, freely expressing one's opinions, opening up to the world, is not a "value", it is normality. That is why we should look at it with a large degree of respect: it is a generation for which sharing, one of the most important values in human relationships, is an inborn characteristic. However the most common interpretation of this approach is often to say that these kids, according to the particular case, are either superficial or narcissistic.

For example, so many people have questioned the way they take selfies and continually post about what they are doing on social networks. All teenagers do indeed spend a lot of time researching the way in which they can show themselves off to others and Millennials did the same, perhaps in an exponential way because of the options that the Internet has been offering them since they were adolescents. But in relation to previous generations, Generation Y has "had to" do it in an authentic way: if it weren't done authentically, they would have been exposed by posts and hashtags.

With Millennials, the value of transparency has developed thanks to the opportunity of being able to talk freely about themselves on blogs, and also thanks to the evidence of having seen a friend publicly "punished", and tagged in a photo which contradicts what he was pretending to be. The chance of rating everything with stars, votes, likes, comments on various opinion and review platforms, or on Facebook, is an enabler of authenticity. Transparency of feedback, authenticity and coherence are thus prerequisites for young people to be able to experience relationships on line.

The transparency that guides Millennials can thus be seen as a result of the relationship dynamics which work in social media: a blog that does not talk an authentic and real language will not have followers; content which is not very credible on a given Facebook page will not get "likes"; a fake user who infiltrates a discussion forum will quickly be unmasked. The Internet has its rules, which govern a solid and cohesive society, which comes together en masse to rectify what other people write, if people don't agree, until a consensus emerges.

So this is the other side of the coin: on the one hand transparency is a strategy to set up relationships and not run the risk of being publicly humiliated – in a network that leaves everything visible – and on the other the transparency of young people stems from their being used to sharing their thoughts, opinions, ratings of something, in very direct terms without filters.

Amongst other things, thanks to these mechanisms, content posted on the Internet by normal people, in the end tends to represent the truth about things to a much greater extent than what a council of elders or jury could do. People talk a lot about the veracity of information on the Internet, starting with the profile that everyone writes about themselves on social networks: "and who says that's true?", "of course, everybody says what best suits them about themselves". But it isn't like that.

Why do they run the risk of being proved wrong, and not simply reflect things as they are or as they think they are? Why not show oneself as one actually is, perhaps emphasising the things in us that we feel most worthy? When the white box under an article asks for your opinion, why not decide not to give it? Why not say what you think when the more information web pages have, the more value they have and create? Why, at the end of the day, shouldn't you be transparent in real life, if you have grown up in a world that asks for, favours and is made up of authentic and transparent contributions? One of Oscar Wilde's sayings goes: "give him a mask and he will tell you the truth". Young people don't need a mask, and it has been the intermediation of the computer to remove the need for that.

The implication of this value for people who do marketing is of fundamental importance: it forces companies to go from a relationship of supremacy with the consumer (because they know what the world will be like, because it is them who set trends, because they have the best product, because they have an important name and so on) to a relationship of equality, which is based on listening, shared values, the uniqueness of viewpoints and the absence of any reputational stain. It also asks for communication to move from an analogical kind of method of diffusion to a dialogue type, through social media and other channels, at every touch point.

Y.es, now!

Keywords: **#immediate #realtime #reaction #hicETnunc #now #ready**

Millennials are the generation of the "here and now", of "everything immediately".

To understand the things that are unusual about this generation compared with young people in the past, we should look at the web, which has caused their imprinting. Using the Internet is like immersing oneself in an overflowing river: it is a flow of information and stimuli that are experienced only if they are captured and frozen with a click. The results of a key word search on Google, for example, change from one moment to another, even though it is the same person to type it from the same computer. A piece of advertising on a given part of a website changes a moment later (the first time the page is refreshed) if we don't click it.

Growing in an environment created by phenomena which change so often and so fast has produced an unusual mindset in terms of reactivity: their brain is programmed to understand the objects in movement, which are to be stopped with a like, or researched further with a click. Living at speed like this is an approach that is almost an anthropological characteristic, the product of a system that adapts to posts that move quickly across social media profiles. It is against invasive pop-ups which should be closed as soon as possible so as to seek out interesting areas on crowded pages. Millennials see the things that surround them in a different way from adults: they see them in movement, so in context.

"I see a lot of young people as part of my professional work," said Professor Michele Oldani, a socio-psychotherapist that I met for the first time in 2015 at a conference on young people[25] *"and the difference is the way in which they see, and how they see us. To give an example: it is like seeing a tree from close up, or when you are standing still in front of it, or seeing it from a bicycle or a train. What's the difference between them? What do I see in each case? In the first I grasp all the elements, the details, but in the second I can see the context, the tree set in what surrounds it and*

---

[25] https://goo.gl/YNHyRD

which thus gives it meaning. Young people today are used to understanding things in their context, both spatial and temporal."

Millennials are quick out of necessity, their approach means they have an all-round view, they are compulsive explorers: using the Internet, letting yourself get carried away with clicks, can lead very far away if you no longer know how to return to the starting point, or if a particular path is not followed. Social networks like Facebook and, still more, Twitter make advertising posts move in front of you uninterruptedly, because the community is always posting. This has the effect that each content lives if it is seen at a given moment since it will become submerged by later posts, and so will actually disappear. That is why a Millennial will immediately click on the "like" button if they like a photo posted by a friend: waiting a moment could mean not being able to find it any more. They behave in the same way when they see an advertising banner which tells them something interesting: if they don't click immediately they can lose out on the promotion, which is the project of a certain combination of luck and browsing habits in the preceding half hour.

It isn't a matter of anxiety or schizophrenia: it is a consequence of their adaptive system. Young people are used to being able to immediately understand what they might find interesting and what not, since the web only stops with the click of a photo. At the same time, brands should immediately understand that a phenomenon is taking place, an event that is happening to Millennials, so as to be able to immediately take action in the conversation that is taking place. There are various examples of companies that have been able to join consumer conversations, leveraging off the trending topic of the moment: a lot of cases are shown here https://goo.gl/N7cjZo .

We can thus say that working quickly is a prerogative for young people which stems from the need to react quickly to stimuli from the web. "Think before acting!", say the Baby Boomer parents; "Actually it is better to act fast, and think while you are doing it", their children from Generation Y might reply, knowing that they will have to acquire all the information needed during the process, not too early, but neither too late.

Immediacy is thus a necessity. But it is also the product of their aspiration to live situations in a direct way, without pauses, without breaks: speed is what means young people can live the moment, the here and now, without reflection; their behaviour is immediate, in that it is not premeditated.

How many times have you seen a young person interrupt at the beginning of an argument, or a dispute on the meaning of a word, or the name of a place or an actor, by looking up the answer on Google or Wikipedia, without giving the others time to think, or to reflect for a bit and try to remember... why wait?

The web has meant that they are used to finding immediate answers to everything or nearly everything, as that is the world they have grown up in: they don't even need to imagine notions any more, because they are always available in very little time by Googling the unknown word or a particular person: Google is the Millennials' memory.

The speed with which information and stimuli flow one after another in an average day for a Millennial, who is always immersed in devices which are always on and involved in multitasking, calls for the highest degree of reactivity to establish the things that they feel are relevant, by taking immediate action, before they disappear. Actions are carried out at the moment that the stimulus arrives and not later, and that is why young people's brains strain to apply themselves to something, to commit things to memory, and work in a "*last in, first out*" way.

We have to deal with this attitude to things, to situations, relationships and advertising.

When I was giving a course on digital communication to bank employees, a director said to me: "Yes but it is absurd that these young people are unlearning everything. I went somewhere with my son and some of his friends. At a certain point I joined their conversation with an innocuous comment: "that's just like what happens in Lisbon". Well, nobody knew where Lisbon was. Can you imagine that? Then you tell me that it is the most informed and educated generation ever?".

The idea of storing information simply doesn't occur to Generation Y. It is all there, readily available in the external memory that they have in their computer or cellphone. It is difficult to accept for us, we who grew up memorising historical events and poetry. But on the other hand, I can't see why we should attribute a moral aspect to it: rather we should say to ourselves that the Millennials are organising themselves to handle the information overload of the modern era.

What is fairly useful to recognise is that rather than endlessly "warehousing information", young people concentrate on the relationship between events. What is worth remembering are the links to be activated to dig out the original meaning of a concept saved in the "portable memory". The way Millennials have grasped this has various implications for marketing, which thus needs to make people recall – in an implicit or explicit way – the points of connection between the messages contained in various different touch points and various communication which have been transmitted on different media.

Michele Oldani, again in his speech on the way that young people see time in the convention mentioned earlier, said: *"We have grown up in a world that asked us to run away from the past, to evolve, to change, to grow... And which looked at the future as a land of opportunity, of progress, or evolution. The present, for us adults, has never been important, on the contrary: focusing too much on the present meant vanity. Young people today, however, mainly look at the present. The past isn't a necessary starting point, and the future is so uncertain that it loses interest."*

For Millennials, past and future converge in the present and collide with it: a photo is taken and at the moment that it is posted, immediately becomes a memory. More than that, it has already been taken as a memory and the moment quickly becomes the past, even before or while we are experiencing it. At the same time, that experience can be lived for ever, and will re-emerge on social media even in the most unexpected ways. The present is always present, it has neither past nor future.

L.iberty

Keywords: #freedom #access #variety #movement #easiness #creativity

It is difficult to explain to an adult the concept of liberty that young people have today. Each generation of young people before the current one has always associated the exercise of freedom with transgression, with the struggle against authority and power: you can find expressions of this in the parent-child conflicts experienced by young people in the past, and in student-teacher struggles, in conflicts between citizens and governments, in the dissent over dominant regulations and customs. For young people, Liberty has always been a value to defend and to fight for through transgression.

As far as Millennials are concerned, freedom is not a human right to be defended, a victory against authority and power: they don't have anything or anyone to oppose. They have grown up in families which are attentive, encouraging, with parents who are not authoritarian but always understanding and loving. The Web, then, has completed the job, providing them every kind of freedom to say, do, think and display themselves.

They have grown up 'surfing' between websites and choosing between the infinite possibilities, developing the extraordinary capacity of entering and then leaving content and relationships in a carefree and fluid way. For them it has always been an alternative path, a "free" way to obtain things, a chance to say what they think, a possibility of making contact with somebody they don't know: they have never felt themselves obliged to choose between opposites and to take positions, their horizon is much broader, their range of options go well beyond black and white, communism or fascism, mathematics or literature. They have grown up being able to experiment in thousands of different worlds, forums and communities: they have learnt that they can be everything, one thing and its opposite. In that sense they are happy: they don't have a brand that will always be their favourite, they aren't dogmatic.

Basically, freedom is a given as far as they are concerned, not something they have to aspire to. A wide range of choice, simple access, the absence of formalisms, and the chance to break free are the manifestations of a Millennial's liberty, a freedom that cannot be really seen as a value, because the concept of wanting freedom is absent for them[26]. Young people don't dream of a free world, they already have one (they don't consider changing a brand that doesn't offer them freedom, they just change brand); they don't do campaigns or demonstrate on the streets, they use the web; they don't get behind a brand, they choose it. Remember the opposition in Generation X between those who drank Coca-Cola and those who liked Pepsi, between those who wore Nike and those who liked Adidas, those who liked McDonald's and those who preferred Burger King, those who liked pop music and those who liked heavy metal? The world of the Millennials doesn't make a choice between two opposites, but works between infinite possibilities and puts together its own preferred option.

For Millennials, freedom means simplified access to the contents of a brand, the chance to choose between variations of product and price, the possibility of expressing and trying out things without restrictions and without taking predetermined positions.

Having a "Millennials Mindset" thus means making the company consumer relationship free, since it is:
- **simple** and lean, so that users can use the products, services, brand contents (*customer experience*) in a way that can be exploited at every possible touch point;
- **open**, without pretending to ask for blind faith or being eternally faithful, without asking the consumer to get behind the brand and against the competition;
- **interconnected**, recognising the value of the consumer for the company and not just the other way round ("I give you a great product, and you pay me"), and stimulating the expression of consumer opinions, allowing them to shape the communication message, the content, the product that is offered to them, opening up to co-creation and co-generated content.

Freedom, for Post Millennial Marketing, is thus not an ethical value to be conveyed through advertising, but a way of relating to the consumer that materialises with what one does: with the breadth of product range and

---

[26] Clyde Kluckhohn: "A value is a concept of the desirability, explicit or implicit, which distinguishes an individual or characterises a group, that influences the choice between possible ways of doing things, means and the object of the action."

customisation, with affordable prices, with highly-usable shops and touch points, with a customer care service with a problem-solving approach, giving a chance for expression and doing activities together.

E.xperience

Keywords: #immersion #emotion #fun #drama #intimate #lean #value

The web has taught young people that it is more important to experience the things that they possess. It has taught them by encouraging them to talk about their experiences: for example in a blog, sharing personal opinions or reflections; or in a forum, making their direct experience of a product benefit the community; or in a social network, taking and posting photos of the moment right as it is being experienced. It is not having things or being in a post that matters, but what is said of it, because that makes the value of what has been experienced grow, for them and for others.

It is thus a generation which is used to paying attention to experiences. Their network of friends is interested in how things were done, the emotions that have been experienced, the sensations that have been felt, it is not so much what has been done, but how. These are the posts that receive the most "likes", since they enable more direct and deep contact with one's own friends, which is shown very clearly in its more emotional side. One learns a lot more and one grows from the experience of others, not just from simple pieces of information.

We could thus say that the web has led the Millennials to concentrate on their experiences because they know that they must talk about them online, but it isn't just that. The web has actually worked in another way in shaping this thirst for experience: the dynamics of using the web, with games, entertainment and interactive communication, have led young people to look for more active relationships with things. Young people have given up passive use, because it is boring and above all not very rewarding; but interaction allows them to immerse themselves in things that mean involvement and greater participation.

That is why people say "they don't ever manage to tear themselves away from their computer or cellphone": as soon as they are browsing they can be completely immersed, looking for an active role in the relationship with content. And that is how they have learnt to use communication media.

Indeed just as soon as they could, they also got their hands on television content, to introduce a bit of customisation and interactive experience: they call it the "second screen" or "social TV". On the sofa, in front of the television and with a cellphone in their hand, they try to create their own viewing experience, thanks to the exchange with other people on Twitter or Facebook, sharing the feelings created by the programme, or communicating directly with the presenter.

Millennials have grown up in a world that has allowed and asked them to share their experiences, and to get the most out of them by using likes and views. But the experience is also what they themselves are looking for in their relationships with others and with brands: that is perhaps what most distinguishes Post Millennial consumers from others.

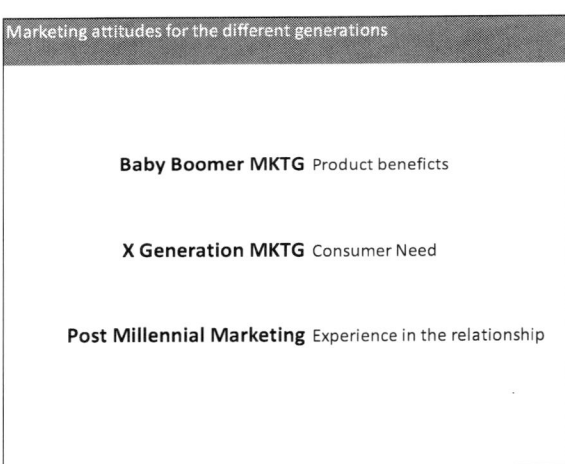

Marketing attitudes for the different generations

Baby Boomer MKTG Product beneficts

X Generation MKTG Consumer Need

Post Millennial Marketing Experience in the relationship

Getting the most out of experience leads the Post Millennial consumer to focus on the service aspect, even in manufactured products. A brand of drink, food, a car and a fridge – each have their own USP (Unique Selling Proposition). This increasingly lies not so much in a product's performance in the strict sense, or in how it positions its image and takes inspiration from a given lifestyle. But it more and more involves the value that it manages to generate in a consumer, before, during or after consuming the goods, through services or benefits deriving from the product.

Post Millennial Marketing sees consumers as clients of a service, in which the delivery of the product is just a single facet. Millennials' search for experience thus takes shape in their opening to embracing the brand in an all-round way, in every possible way in which it manages to create a benefit for the client. Even more so now that the sharing economy promises to make us give up our desire to own and instead to embrace the use of things in a shared way: the Post Millennial consumer wants experiences and services from brands, and no longer ownership to be displayed or consumed.

How many Millennials?

It is difficult to believe that a generation could be a single entity and that inside it everyone is all the same in terms of profile, character and – above all – in what the implications are for marketing: the habits, the family provenance and attributes (cultural and technological) of every one have an impact when we see them as targets for our companies. Actually, even though the traits which have been described up to now are essentially stable and shared by the whole generation, various pieces of research show how, for marketing, a distinction should nevertheless be made between one Millennial and another. It is worth repeating so as to eliminate any risk of misunderstanding: the value traits of the Millennials, the S.T.Y.L.E. that we will see in a few pages, are stable and shared by the whole generation: it is just a matter of understanding the various different segments to put together more specific marketing strategies and more detailed segmentation in relation to the product and brand.

Recent research carried out by Kantar TNS and Kantar Millward Brown for Ceres[27], has identified five 5 sub-groups within 16-35 year-old Millennials: we will refer to this research and look deeper into the description of the various types.

Pin-pointed = pragmatic, with a clear need and aim to find a space in this world, and with a strong interest that catalyses their energies.

Indie Alternative = full of passions, including creative ones, autonomous and non-conformist thinker, social but also able to derive benefit from moments alone.

Pop-Fellow = straightforward, sunny disposition, sociable, finds his or her ideal dimension in groups and in slightly escapist entertainment

---

[27] By kind permission of the Company.

One (Wo)Man Show = extrovert and sociable, focused on themselves and especially their image, seeking out everything that can give them visibility

Party guy = dynamic, hyperactive, very attentive to what happens in the time and place that they inhabit, driven by the desire to "be there"

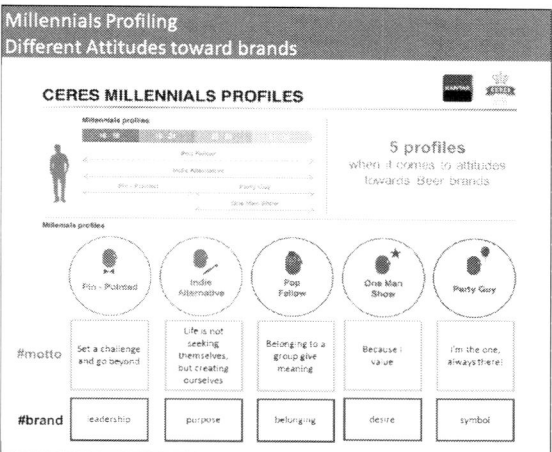

There are various kinds of profile that brands interested in Millennials can make their target. The implications in terms of brand and communication can actually be different according to the sub-profiles with which they intend to relate: the brand could play a different role in the relationship, according to which kind of Millennial they find themselves faced with.

Chapter V – THE FUTURE: POST MILLENNIAL MARKETING

"Millennialism" is not just following a new target

Whether there are a lot of them or just a few, whether they are rich or poor, if they are able to destroy the online reputation of a brand with a single post or whether they really don't care about our product, Millennials are an extremely interesting and useful target for marketing people. For everybody, with no exceptions, including those who work in old countries like Italy, and even for those who make products for old people.

Millennials must interest us because they are the most likely picture of our near future. They interest us because through them we will understand how our consumers will think in a few years' time, because we will learn how to do marketing in a different and innovative way. And they interest us because they stimulate and provoke us, with marketing in the middle of a process of change that is not just a good thing, but also – and most of all – necessary.

Every so often, when the companies with which I work meet Millennials, I hear myself saying: "well, they aren't that different from us". That phrase simultaneously hides both something true, and something false. If we refer to the use of digital devices, actually, even though they are apparently similar to people older than them, young people from this generation have a very different approach to the digital world after all: the ways with which they use the devices, the motivations and the experience that they have with respect to them is profoundly different, even though both adults and young people are always connected nowadays.

A "digital native" can be incredibly similar to a "digital immigrant" because of the number of times that each of them connects to the Internet, because of the devices they have, the sites that they use, the services that they look up. But for adults technology is a means, whereas for Millennials it is completely transparent. So you don't just need familiarity with technology to be a Millennial; to be a Millennial you need to adhere to a particular value system, which is the S.T.Y.L.E, and to have lived through the social, economic and technological transformation of the Web 2.0. as an adolescent. The demographic aspect isn't the only requirement, as we have said many times, but you can't have an old person who is also a Millennial (not even in spirit, as is often said…), for the simple reason that they grew up in a very different world.

On the other hand, the statement "they aren't actually that different from us" which one sometimes hears in the business community, and which could mean that they recognise themselves in Millennials, is then not so very wrong because of other aspects. The marketing community, because of its exposed nature and the fact that it is influenced by trends in society, has actually been involved, more than others in these very same disruptive revolutions which the Millennials have generated, and has thus already changed a bit, but of course before other population segments.

The fact that a marketing director says he is more similar to his daughter than his father was to him is at the same time true, in that we are talking about a cultural and technological elite who have begun "Millenialisation" before anyone else; but on the other hand it brings to light a great misunderstanding which comes from the absence of a real "break" or revolution between Generations X and Y: the change isn't so visible or explicit as it was in the past, the passage between one generation and another is more in ideas than behaviour, and consequently they sometimes seem very similar to us.

That means that studying Millennials and aiming part of our activity at them, whether a lot or a little depending on the relevance of the segment to company results, is strategic:

- We target the elite of our society, not the technological elite, but the elite of the emerging culture of collaboration, of positive globalisation, of transparency in relationships, of the immediacy of action, of the here and now, of immersion in the context (so essentially of the S.T.Y.L.E)

- We should learn the new paradigms of marketing and communication that our company will be called upon to adopt in the near future: we can learn how to communicate from Millennials.

Essentially, studying Millennials is like having a living observatory on the future and taking action to involve them is a bit like working out in the gym to prepare yourself for what will happen. Only if you don't have any Millennials amongst your consumers, only if you feel that no community of Millennials could dent your reputation, only if you think that no Millennial will ever buy your product, not even in thirty years' time... then only in that case should you consider whether or not to do these gym exercises for the future. But in all other cases a marketing plan for Millennials should be prepared. That is really the reason why the word "Millennial" is currently such a key term at so many conferences, and in so many sectors, from food to banking.

So, if we refer to the story of the fish we mentioned earlier, you have to immerse yourself to understand how people live under water, it is not enough to just get your ankles wet (and perhaps get out quickly because the water feels too cold…)!

This book is called "Post Millennial Marketing" precisely because of that, because the world changed at a certain time, and with it we are all destined to change.

How marketing will change: implications of the S.T.Y.L.E.

One of the base parameters for a fruitful relationship between a brand and Millennials is adherence to the same system of values: if for a Baby Boomer a brand had to represent a chance for social or cultural advancement; if for Generation X the brand represented a system of values to be aimed at; then for Millennials the brand has to represent an authentic world that is in line with the one wanted by consumers themselves. Essentially, for Millennials a brand or product will likely be amongst their favourites if it is something they identify with, not if it is something they should aspire to be.

The Millennial generation has a very different character from Generation X and the Baby Boomers, since it is inspired by different values. Let's try to compare the values of the three generations, through the keywords we have already listed in preceding pages:

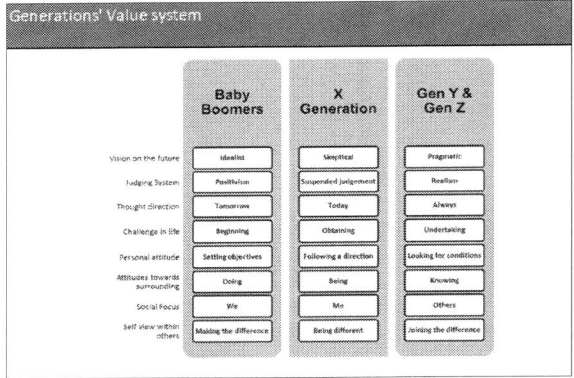

Baby Boomer, Generation X and Millennials are actually based on (have been created by) different value systems; so in the same way, the visions and tools of marketing used to understand, attract and satisfy each of them must be different.

Following the values of the three generations, the brands should give themselves different roles, different missions in their relationship with consumers.

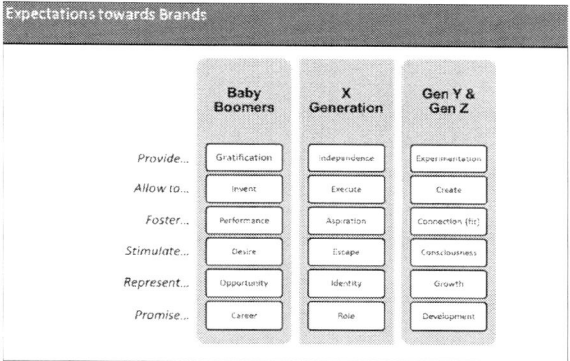

To connect with Millennials, marketing must be in tune with their value system: essentially it must have the same S.T.Y.L.E. as them:

- **S - Sociability**: if it can, the post-Millennial brand creates and stimulates getting together around a passion, an interest, or even a product itself; it advertises, but through that it creates a chance for socialising, and it doesn't broadcast a television advert aimed at "doing everything" in 30 seconds. Communication media are transparent, giving visibility to content and favouring the different connections between points of contact. Companies with S.T.Y.L.E. carry out market research with observational methods integrated with engaging interactive sessions, aimed at co-creation and at development in a participatory way.

- **T - Trasparency**: post-Millennial marketing doesn't go in for propaganda, but rather has a dialogue, making its aims clear, admitting its errors if that is the case, and seeking approval or disapproval to continually improve; the post-Millennial brand doesn't seek fleeting relationships and "dark patterns[28]" but talks of itself in an honest way, getting the most out of its own history and people, and explaining – where necessary – the reasoning behind strategic choices.

- **Y – Yes, now!**: the post-Millennial brand experiences the context and intervenes to give its own interpretation of current events that it considers most relevant to the values that inspires it. In the same way, it puts forward concrete projects and reacts quickly if it senses aversion from its customers, even though it is not dominated by this: the post-Millennial brand lives the current day and doesn't necessarily follow individualisms or fashions. The post-Millennial brand is anchored to its values, it doesn't forget them: it lives the present, but allows its past to re-emerge, put into context and revisited, so it doesn't hide in the past, but neither does it hide from it.

- **L - Liberty**: the post-Millennial brand doesn't insist on loyalty, it doesn't ask for long-term promises, it doesn't fence in the consumer, but accepts severe assessment on the field and wins loyalty day after day, accepting provisional desertions only to give itself the aim of reconquest; the post-Millennial brand supplies products, services, communication (websites!) which are accessible and usable. The post-Millennial company offers options and puts together packages, it doesn't project "one size fits all" solutions.

- **E - Experience**: the post-Millennial brand goes from seller to publisher, providing – both in digital and non-digital environments – emotions, games, entertainment in a personalised way, content in which the very act of choosing and consuming itself becomes a moment of complete immersion in the brand system. Post-Millennial communication seeks interaction, explicit involvement, likes and shares; it seeks to bring out, excite, to come into contact with the area of personal, social and cultural

---

[28] These are the "tricks" used to encourage users to click on a page or sign up for membership with the user's active awareness: www.darkpatterns.org

relevance to its consumers. The post-Millennial brand makes people grow, assimilate and learn. The post-Millennial brand takes care and enriches the experience with the brand at every touch point, managing those that are owned and influencing those that have been made by others (User Generated Content), where possible.

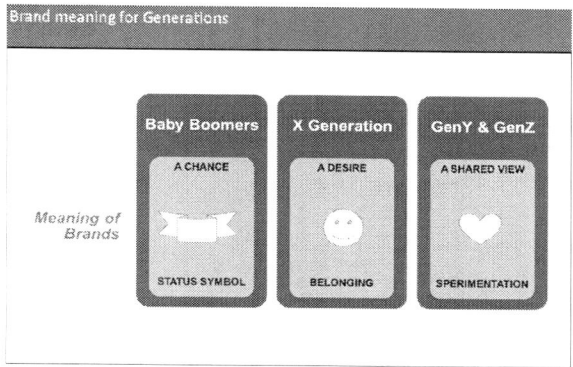

In summary, to have the same S.T.Y.L.E. as the Millennials, a brand must be:
- a chance to share, or at least it must provide stimuli to sharing, it must offer networking opportunities, it has to interpret relationships and production in a collaborative way;
- transparent and authentic, seeking dialogue, inspiring loyalty, being open to assessment from its consumers, and seek feedback;
- reactive, contextual, current, but must also accept being volatile, and living the present, the here and now without any yearning for eternity;
- accessible, multi-faceted, aimed at diversity, and providing escapism rather than trying to block change or even the challenge of a competitor;
- a pleasing experience, one with impact that is memorable because it is immersive and personalised.

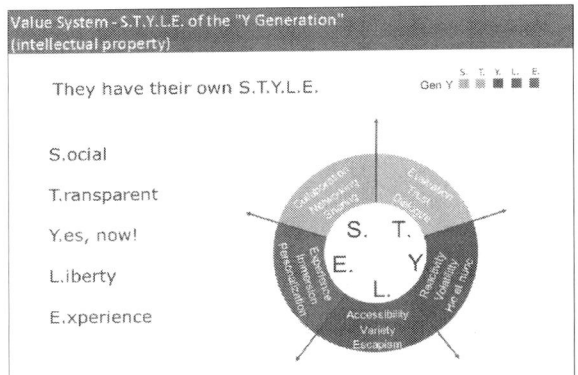

And the brand of the Centennials? As we have said, the Centennials are an offshoot of the Millennials: making the values above their own, they have the same expectations of brands, but their S.T.Y.L.E. varies to give a more concrete, balanced and aware outlook.

For Generation Z:

- being social means moving in small groups which are picked for specific aims of conversation, not expecting to always talk to everybody in a "one to many" way, as often happens with posts on social networks;
- transparency means calling a spade a spade, being straightforward, getting right to the point and being pragmatic;
- being immediate means being up to date on what happens and living the present in its newest and most trend-setting expressions;
- being free means being able to have an impact on things, to affect the context without restrictions or delay;
- looking for experiences means looking for a chance to grow, train and learn.

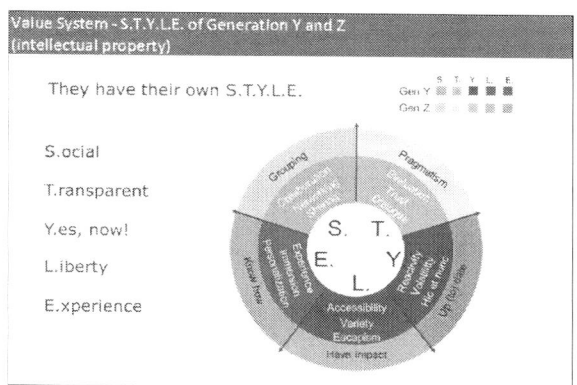

"Centennials are growing up with a less idealistic and more pragmatic feel. They are faced by a situation that the Millennials didn't have to face until they were adults, and consequently Centennials are growing up more solid and expert, in much harder times, when nobody wins, when choices are limited, and success is more difficult to achieve."[29]

---

[29] Kantar Futures research: http://thefuturescompany.com/centennials-infographic/

The brands most recognised by Millennials thus practise S.T.Y.L.E:

S.ociability	Nike	Nike gives runners the chance to always be connected and to make their sports activities sociable, connecting people around a shared passion, allowing virtual and physical meetings, leveraging and building a sense of community.
	7-Eleven	7-Eleven in Indonesia has transformed its chain of shops into places where young people can meet up, providing hot food and open-air locations on local lines, as well as free WiFi and encouraging live music amongst customers.
T.ransparency	GAP	The GAP "Dress normal" campaign was very successful with Millennials (less so with other segments of the population). It focusses on the feeling of freedom generated by not striving to be special and original at all costs.
	Domino's	In 2009 Domino's answered negative feedback on its pizzas which started to go viral, by reviewing its recipes and at the same time putting out the 'Our Pizza Sucks' campaign: sales grew 233% in two years, compared with 37% at its main competitor.
I.mmediacy	ZipCar	Zipcar, Spotify, Uber and Velocity are examples of how some brands manage to give Millennial consumers what they want instantly, or in a very short timeframe.
	Ceres	Coca-Cola, Oreo, McDonalds, Tide, Oreo, Barilla and other giants organise "war rooms" during large events so as to be able to follow, react and offer content, messages and provocations in line with the trending topics of the moment. An interesting case is that of Ceres, which uses its social channels to mock politicians and to insert itself in a debunking way in current affairs. The best example of this is the #SanremoCeres initiative: the brand hired the balcony of the house next to the Ariston theatre to comment on the most famous Italian music festival and put forward its own User-Generated version[30].

---

[30] https://jcp.im/2016/02/10/sanremoceres-i-geni-di-ceres-e-il-loro-balcone-a-sanremo2016/

Liberty	Red Bull	The freedom of doing and expressing yourself to the maximum is the aim of Red Bull's communication, not the product in a strict sense. The aim of the brand is to give a platform to the courage of its customers, and this has come over time to be a source of additional business for the company, since Red Bull is now a media content producer of alternative and extreme sport.
	Burger King	"Hello McDonald's. We come in peace" is the beginning of the Burger King initiative for peace day, when it invites its customers to ask its arch enemy to also sell the "McWapper", a sandwich with the ingredients of both brands, in their outlets.
E.sperience	Apple	Named Apple Seamless Experience, it is the architecture of the user experience system aimed at providing the user with the simplest and most pleasing experience in every point of contact with the brand, from store design to staff, the e-commerce product delivery system, product usability and customer.
	Airbnb	As well as a detailed reservation management system, services to stop fraud, evaluation of both the experience and the stay participants (guests and hosts), Airbnb understands that Millennials feel that a journey is an experience of discovery, of getting to know other people and oneself, and that is why it plans its communication, social spaces, reviews and blogs around this feeling.

We could quote a lot of other examples and cases of successful initiatives: you just have to use any search engine to find hundreds of them, with different variations according to the viewpoint and the area of expertise that the person who has gathered them wanted to emphasise. As in the case of those selected above, the most successful brands have aimed at one or two elements of Millennials' S.T.Y.L.E: product, communication, service model, shopping experience and even the way prices are set have elements of sociability, transparency, immediacy, liberty and overall care of the experience.

There are a lot of points in common between Generation Y and Generation X – and in this book the term Millennials is often used in an expanded way, including both in the same typological group – but there are also significant differences, owing to the different historical moments at which they were born and grew up: Generation Y, which saw a generational rupture, which entered the future without witnesses, is much more idealist than Generation Z, which was formed during the economic recession, and seems a lot firmer, pragmatic and aware, including in its approach to the web.

Specifically regarding initiatives for Generation Z, there is a case that seems particularly emblematic: the Sky Academy Studios, an initiative aimed at kids from 8 to 16 which hosts schools, upon request, for half a day designed to give young people a taste of being backstage at SKY.

The programme includes visiting the television studios and the young people, working as a team, can create real journalism to broadcast, in which each child plays the role of a television professional. This programme had a lot of success since its first year, and has brought thousands of students to the SKY headquarters of the television broadcaster without needing to spend large amounts on advertising and marketing, but just through the strength of the concept and its S.T.Y.L.E, which is interpreted in a special way by Generation Z:

Gen Z Feature	SKY Academy
S.ociability "Small Groups"	Classes take part, so the children's everyday restricted environment, and they then get together to work in further micro-groups.
T.ransparency "Pragmatism"	The initiative shows, in a very practical way, what happens backstage at the television channel, revealing its secrets and removing the mask of superficiality in television: one of the explicit aims of the initiative is actually to help the kids adopt a critical approach to information (Media Literacy).
Y.es, now! "up (to) date"	In just a half day, the kids can put together a journalistic programme, dealing with current social issues that they face at school, and see it prepared for a real broadcast.
L.iberty "being able to impact"	Each child chooses to play a specific role within the group and in relation to what is prepared, learning more about what it entails and the skills needed, from producer to director, up to presenter and cameraman.
E.xperience "Growth and know-how"	The entire initiative has been conceived to create awareness of how television works amongst the children and to develop team-working skills, creativity, communication and problem solving.

The Post Millennial Marketing framework

Marketers for Generation X had a framework in mind when they tackled a marketing plan: AIDA. It was a process of building an interconnected communication plan in four steps, which was to take brand to success:
- create Awareness (or Attention)
- stimulate Interest
- generate Desire
- lead to Action (or Purchase)

According to this model, there are four essential foundations to (advertising) communication, which should be met in a logical sequence:

1. Advertising must above all get itself noticed and generate **awareness** for the product or brand
2. Once the consumer's attention is won, it is fundamental to create **interest**, to make the audience dwell upon the message
3. Advertising needs to begin the process of creating **desire** in consumers, so that they feel an unstoppable impulse to buy it
4. The last step is the **action** (or purchase): advertising needs to lead to action, the message needs to get people to do something.

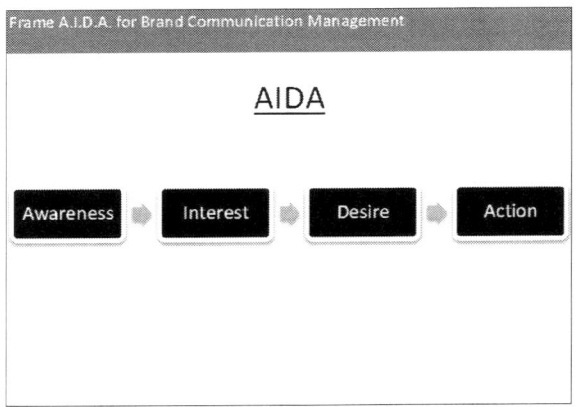

In marketing plans and in the choice of media, subsequent activation was thus considered, according to the specific stage (aim) of the brand-target relationship: advertising could be done (on television) to generate awareness, then press advertising would explain the product, or a sampling event could let it be tried. After the activity focussing on definite targets out (in order to generate product desire) was carried, mainly using advertising, the point of sales would them be worked on. According to shopper marketing analysis, this would stimulate purchase while shoppers were shopping. Seen the other way round, every act of communication could have the aim of making the brand or product known, or of generating interest through its promises and benefits, and could be called on to talk to the most emotional and intimate sphere or to enhance the call to action in a more concrete way.

Many people feel that this model doesn't work any more, for two types of reason: on the one hand, following an explosion in the number of touch points and the amount of communication, it seems too mechanical; on the other its sequentiality has been questioned, as being not sufficiently realistic, if we consider some recent marketing successes: brands created and which have become cult before (or without) investing in advertising; those with formidable brand awareness that give way in terms of trust to supermarket brands; decisions that take place directly at the point of sale, without having a pre-constituted "Top of Mind" brought from home.

The dynamics of choice in digital systems, which have determined the Millennial mindset, have contributed to confirm a rather different consumer journey, from many different points of view: more points of contact, new interaction and a new mindset in making choices.

Indeed Generation X absorbed advertising and was really able to create an association between needs and brands, which was so strong as to stay intact up to the point of sale; but Millennials, when they have a brand in mind, put it up for discussion in a natural way, without judging it or through bad intentions: they google the preferred product (or even brand) and from there they set off to compare the brand, product characteristics and price with the thousands of other ideas that Internet is able to provide.

"Brand consideration" dynamics: Generation X VS Generation Y

Generation X	Generation Y
need	need
brand association	research
memory	evaluation
purchase	purchase

The Generation X marketer had the aim of entering into the magic field of consideration (the basket made up by two to three preferred brands between which the consumer would have chosen once he or she had got to the point of sale); by contrast, Millennial marketers have the aim of making themselves sought after and making themselves be suggested by algorithms and by friends of the consumer. "Perhaps you were looking for...", or "other people like you have also seen...", or even "put this in your trolley as well...": it is the world that has shaped the Millennials' cognitive system, that is why the way they choose is an iterative process and doesn't (just) depend on Top of Mind acquired with GRPs. In the first case, the first brand that comes to mind is that which will very probably be bought; in the second case, the first brand which comes to mind is simply that which will be used as a keyword in searching.

So the marketing planning process has changed because of a fundamental aspect of Millennial consumers: their interactivity and the connection between users, objects, concepts. That is why marketing doesn't work if we think that consumers are a target to be stimulated by our activities and to be led home using our stimuli. Post Millennial Marketing doesn't stimulate, it lets itself be stimulated by the consumer and by the context, to emerge as the most opportune solution to the case in question.

The Post Millennial Marketing model is based on six pillars, which are not steps to be taken in sequence, but activities to be done in a continuous way and often at the same time:

- **Listen to markets** (listen to markets and consumers pro-actively): look for consumers, don't wait for them to look for you
- **Pop-up in moments** (which appear at specific moments): selects and enters at times that are relevant to the consumer
- **Surprise with contents**: creates surprise, it should abandon conformism and allow consumers to do the same
- **Facilitate Action**: explains the aim, the cause and makes the action easier/ accessible
- **Enrich Experience** (enriches touch points with experience): this enlarges individual experience pre/during/post-purchase, using touch points which can influence satisfaction and reputation
- **Connect with Brand Purpose** (connect with the brand and the role that it has for the consumer): reconnects all the touch points and the

individual expressions with the universal values of the brand, its identity and the role to the consumer which it gives itself.

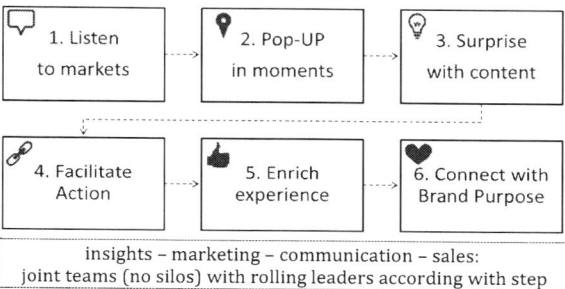

Listen to markets

Marketing has never been able to do without market research: a marketing plan starts from an understanding of what consumers need, of market segments, of habits of exploiting communication media, of purchase intentions. Traditionally, to get a detailed understanding of a consumer, the following are used in both personal and digital execution:

- quantitative type methods: data gathered from large samples through questionnaires which are analysed with statistical-mathematical types of technique;
- qualitative type methods: information gathered through in-depth individual interviews or focus groups, analysed using psychological or sociological kinds of technique;
- observational type methods: evidence gathered passively from the observation of phenomena and behaviour, analysed using ethnographical and behavioural type techniques.

Everything that can be done now is really so much more than just interviewing people: even without asking them to, Millennials (and not just them, from post-Millennialism onwards) talk about themselves, of what they are doing, of how they are doing it, of what they love and what they hate. They talk about brands, advertising, products they buy and the service that they receive. They talk, write, post, photograph and upload videos. And then they give likes, rankings, shares and comment. Finally they look around the Internet, click, and get to content of various types. Big Data refers to, amongst other things, web usage behaviour and data, and transactional data, as well as that collected by CRM and company management systems: nowadays there is so much information available because of the connection that consumers have with digital devices. Post Millennial market research projects thus follow consumers through the traces that they leave of themselves at the various touch points, they listen to all their opinions, monitor and record their behaviour and activate specific survey-based focus research groups when necessary.

If on the one hand this multiplicity and diversity of sources from which to source data logically represents an opportunity to collect it as soon and as well as possible, on the other hand it means that the company has to face quite a few management challenges.

There are, however, various areas in Big Data management where skills are lacking.

- there are skills and competencies relating to the ability to manage and analyse all this data, which is so varied and dynamic;
- there are complications relating to the IT infrastructure which can host the data and manage it in an integrated way related to the systems which are now present in companies;
- there is still a lack of consensus on how to manage this enormous mass of data and on the best organisational methods to generate competitive value: for example, is it a unit that reports to marketing, to IT, or a new independent function?

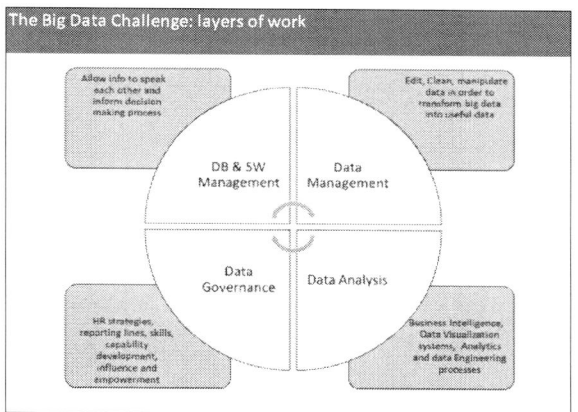

That said, the idea that the availability of this data should be exploited in some way is now broadly accepted, even though there is no intelligent integration of the various ways of doing it, which are not always (up to now) possible because of the volume, variety and speed[31] of the data in

---

[31] Volume, Variety and Velocity are the three Vs that characterise Big Data according to one of the first definitions provided by Gartner in 2001. The

question, which are spread across different databases, in different formats and are often not as complete as we would like.

One of the analysis methods that Post Millennial Marketing has adopted with success is the integration between the analysis of the large amount of behavioural data now available, and which is registered from passive observation, and market research data. By behavioural data we mean both purchase data and transactional data, and also those held on CRM systems, both of web usage and of digital behaviour of the audience, which the company has in it possession. This data can be produced by third parties, when it is detected and managed – by, for example, market research agencies or retailers themselves – or be proprietary data, when data harvesting is carried out by company systems, which have the direct responsibility and ownership of the data itself.

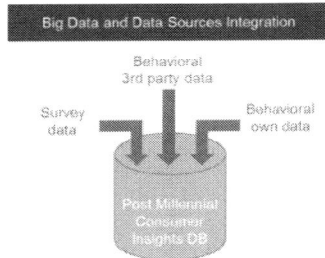

Data which come from the passive measurement of digital behaviour is information gathered in every interaction the user has with a digital object, whether it be a web page, visiting social networks, a comment on social media, using an app, seeing display or non-display advertising content, queries on search engines or geo-localisation data.

The behavioural data that are held in company marketing databases, however, include transaction and purchasing data (the company's own, or those owned by third parties like sell-out data), visits to the store, access to

---

original article by META, which is now part of Gartner, can be found here: https://goo.gl/kdzU5i

company digital property, the redemption of one-to-one campaigns, profiling, P&L financial data of the brand, products, variants, shops, etc. These are the data that Post Millennial companies use to activate detailed segmentation and consequently direct marketing campaigns, for example.

However, after being gathered and registered, the data is very often only used for marketing in a minimal way.

What is the purpose of all this data? There are a large number of concrete applications of the concept of Big Data in marketing: DMP for digital advertising planning, segmentation analysis of the customer database, segmentation to activate marketing automation with anti-churn or upselling goals, sentiment analysis to understand the reputational risk or to manage customer care in the social channels, etc. This is not the place to cover all the possible applications of Big Data to marketing and those listed above are just a few examples. What is interesting is the adherence to the underlying concept: Post Millennial Marketing uses data in an active way, accessing all those available and connecting the various different sources.

With the growing use of social media by consumers and after some success in terms of the virality and popularity of its brands on the web, Nestlé decided to set up a Digital Acceleration Team (DAT) in various different countries where the food giant is present[32]. The team is working on a digital transformation programme which is made up of three basic disciplines – Listening, Engaging, Inspiring & Transforming – to spread the culture and the tools to listen to consumers, to communicate and have a dialogue with social media environments, and to promote internal transformation in the way marketing is done.

In particular, data gathered on the Internet is now a precious insight which allows the Nestlé teams to capture the trends of the moment, understand users' needs, creating personal relationships with customers and stimulating internal innovation following a truly consumer-centric approach.

The Nestlé DAT takes shape in a room in which data analysis software is installed, and which has screens for viewing. It can be accessed by anybody at any time so they can become used to working with the data, to

---

[32] There is a video on Youtube called "Digital Trasformation at Nestlé" which shows the unit (www.youtube.com/watch?v=Ib7az5UWF44) and other videos on the various different openings in other countries (www.youtube.com/watch?v=ktsMa8hfgY0&t=118s)

browse or to let themselves be inspired by customers' posts. But it is also to understand how to handle a conversation with one's own users in an engaging way which is personalised for every brand.

The DAT listening platforms are also interrogated by the Business Units whose task it is to handle insights, and by research and marketing consultants, so as to complete the analyses done on consumers with more traditional methods, or to have the first recognition of the key phenomena which need to be looked at more closely.

"The digital room dedicated to the analysis of Internet information," says Walter Scieghi, Head of Marketing & Consumer Communication at Nestlé Italiana on the subject of DAT - *"allows us to create an increasingly personalised relationship with our customers. We actually want to create a relationship of trust which goes beyond the products and which allows us to listen to criticisms and praise, to continue to improve, and to improve people's lives through our products and services."*

The customer listening process should thus integrate traditional analysis techniques or survey-based types with passive behavioural data sources from the Internet or internal sources: market research will allow us to learn the thoughts of consumers, why they buy something, their perceptions and the most qualitative profiling; whereas behavioural data sources will provide actual behaviour, preferred routes, purchase preferences, habits in using communication media and using shops. Survey and behavioural data are two sides of the same coin, and are thus two views that need to be integrated to have a detailed vision of consumers, of their needs and their potential value.

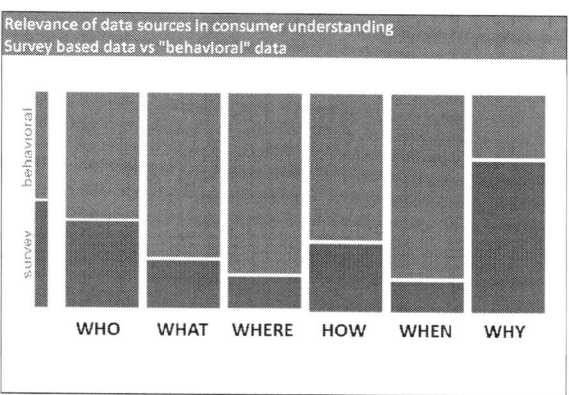

Skilled Big Data management and the integration of the various different sources available allow the activities, preferences and intentions of consumers to be monitored so as to be able to seize opportunities for growing a business or to anticipate the most dangerous, imminent or hidden dangers.

That is why data management, seen from that viewpoint, is not limited to market research: it is a discipline that observes, explores, connects and understands the significance of the data which emerges from the large number of brand touch points, to become activated in response to consumers, to their requests and questions which are set to emerge. **It is active - or rather proactive – listening activity, and is one of many available today.**

Over time, the market research function in many companies has ended up taking on the role of data buyer: it is an office to intermediate between the needs of the company and what is available on the market. Post Millennial Marketing imposes a new role, which is much more strategic in relation to the Consumer Insights function. This function has to be able to **generate insights through the use of diverse type of sources and data. This function needs to be carried out in proactively: at the same time listening** and allowing marketing teams be stimulated by customers, real time.

It is not just a question of sources of analysis that one can have available: overall it is a question of having somebody in the company who is in charge of listening to customers who is thus able to proactively listen to clients (letting themselves be guided by what they observe and not by the marketing needs of the moment). They should be equipped with the ability to influence and to communicate data internally to both marketing colleagues, and also company top management. The ideal profile for the Consumer Insights Director includes both hard skills, in other words the necessary specialist skills, from psychology to statistics, from sociology to IT, and also soft skills, such as communication ability, a team-working approach and creative thinking. The Director of Market Research at a company which deals with Post Millennial Marketing, is actually a Data & Insights Management Director.

Pop-up in moments

Pre Millennials Marketing is aimed at persuading through the projection of aspirational value systems: it knows consumers and tries to influence them using their most fundamental stimuli. But Post Millennial Marketing, needs to change viewpoint and direction: it doesn't show an ideal world, but instead puts forward its own way of being, its own values to try to find a relationship; it doesn't try to stimulate consumers, but is stimulated by them; it doesn't await them at the point of sale, but goes into their homes and takes part in their lives; it doesn't suggest a purchase to them, it incites it; it doesn't talk, it listens.

"We know that you've only got an hour between the spinning class and the 9 o'clock meeting with your boss's boss": that is how Stowaway Cosmetics[33] promotes its simple, small-size product line, calling them *"the right solutions for your busy life"*.

Millennials have grown up at a time in which you talk to brands, you get answers from them, you can watch them and follow them on a daily basis. On the other hand, the same Millennials have grown up being tempted by brands that pay attention to them, which are even flattered by a "follow": for some time now, it has been (or should have been) brands that follow the consumers and no longer the other way round, which is what used to happen with cult brands which were status symbols. Digital, mobile and social technologies have led the way in allowing companies to opt for new communication and relationship models aimed at focusing on the user: contextual advertising, adverts that fit in with detected behaviour; purchases suggested by probabilistic algorithms based on similar groups of users and action; immediate replies on multiple chances of contact; customised purchases through ultra-flexible configurators.

Consumers can just live normally and await the best offer, in the best place at the best price. The technological support available is not yet such as to allow this level of perfection, if the truth be told, but the move from the marketing 1.0 system to the 2.0 type has already been clear for a while. The Post Millennial brand can no longer expect to occupy a pre-defined space within a film, on the edge of a football pitch, next to a supermarket and wait (and hope) that consumers take note of them: the Post Millennial brand doesn't communicate, but appears in specific moments, right at the

---

[33] https://stowawaycosmetics.com/

time which maximises the chance of the marketing work succeeding, since they are the right moments in terms of context and content.

This change of approach in marketing planning is relevant: before digital opportunities you had to put together broad audiences in defined segments to be able to "shoot at the crowd", and thus get the greatest number of users. We can now view things using a very different approach, and plan contact operations following computational logic: a piece of information corresponds to every event generated by the consumers which, if registered, means that know-how can be put together which is useful in programming the activity sequence: Post Millennium marketing makes use of engineering rationale as well as economics, statistical, psychological and social approaches.

The events which we are talking about can be of various different types: they are moments, occasions or situations in which consumers show themselves within a specific context, in which we can make a need appear, or a state of mind, a predisposition to use or to buy, together with their consumption and personal profile. It is at those moments that the brand should appear, appearing as the most natural thing inside that specific context. It can be a website, a specific occasion, a question on a search engine, a presence in a given place: being there at that time goes to inform the marketing system that receives the communication that a favourable event has occurred.

With regard to this, we can say that the choices between media in marketing planning anticipate those of creativity: Generation X marketing looked at the best creative concept and then spelled it out in the various communication media, which were chosen according to the attitude and habits of the client; but Post Millennial Marketing defines content according to the moments.

One example stands out above all: Generation X marketing promotes a mortgage in the branch, or with advertising which was broadcast at a time when it was probable that they would find young couples; Post Millennial Marketing, on the other hand, says that information about the mortgage should appear on websites about houses that are for sale, about weddings and children, and to users who in the past have looked for, talked about, or clicked on content relating to mortgages. An online campaign to promote a mortgage, for example, is more effective when it appears within a discussion forum on organising weddings. Perhaps in the evening when the future couple are together, managing to promote contents in line with the user and his or her needs, since cookies and past surveys – to him or her personally, or to similar people [34] - or their posts on social media have helped in knowing them well.

That is why I would talk of marketing engineering: it is a real programming system that envisages a communicative action in relation to given information on the ecosystem in which users find themselves. It should be noted that this "computational" acceptance of communication activity does not reject the power of creativity, on the contrary: as we will shortly see, it is rather a matter of a different system of reasoning, which leads advertisers to no longer abstractly reflect on consumers and their desires (insights), but on possible combinations of the moment, profiles and needs.

Until the point when technology doesn't allow us to monitor moments, person by person, and to return what a computational algorithm thinks is the best content for the combination of all factors, it will nevertheless be necessary to make use of resourcefulness and practical sense.

From the framework shown above on "moments by profiles by needs", we can actually identify hypotheses of environments in which creativity can be allowed to exist. Uber and Spotify, for example, have come up with a partnership which allows users to find their own preferred playlist when they enter a car. This has the most targeted advertising possible, which can show, through the Spotify data platform and the combination with information gathered from smartphone use, the user's preferences at that very moment.

After having listened to consumers through all the possible means mentioned in the previous section, and after having observed them very widely, we will be able to come up with a system of connections between the various "relevant moments" - or the situations, the occasions and the moments when the capacity that the brand has to relate to the consumer is at its peak – and thus to programme marketing activities in a detailed way, in relation to the performance of actions already carried out on the same individual. In summary, marketing activities should be planned in

---

[34] There are some techniques based on statistics ("look alike" models) that make it possible to extrapolate facts collected on a sample of people to an audience that is much wider but extremely similar because of its intrinsic characteristics.

accordance with the specific moment, the specific customer profile and the consequent (and specific) need that underlies each.

Table for planning moment by profile by need					
	Relevant Moment 1	Relevant Moment 2	Relevant Moment 3	Relevant Moment 4	Relevant Moment 5
Profile A	Need A1	Need A2	Need A3	Need A4	Need A5
Profile B	Need B1	Need B2	Need B3	Need B4	Need B5
Profile ...					

As we are writing this text, the traceability system of the "moments" is only applicable to some digital environments: marketing initiatives can be programmed for these in a fairly effective way, provided that not just the behavioural variables are inserted into the forecasting models, but also those relating to the profile and needs of the consumers.

As has been said, to really understand the opportunities of the market, you have to know how to receive the various different nuances that the consumer gives you, and to systemise the knowledge acquired from his or her past behaviour, from the understanding of the socio-demographic and psychological profile, together with the ability to appreciate basic needs, including those which are not (yet) expressed and those which cannot be made explicit.

In relation to this, the judgement of Douglas Rushkoff is clear and harsh on the recent fascination for analysis carried out on behavioural data, and on the use that marketing makes of this information:

*"However invasive the technology used can be, experts in marketing, surveys and analysis don't ever get to reveal the processes by which people buy or vote: they limit themselves to observing what is bought or thought, and they entrust themselves to data gathered from things that have happened, trying to understand a **"now" that says nothing about desires, motivations or contexts**: it is a simple attempt to put a perimeter around and analyse what we have just done, so as to manipulate our future decisions."* [35]

The identification of the insight on the consumer thus takes place through analysing what happens (relevant moment: context, place, moment,

---

[35] "Present Shock: When Everything Happens Now" by Douglas Rushkoff, 2013

situation, ...), the subject (profile in terms of descriptive and psychological explanatory variables) and the stimuli which could unleash possible interest towards the brand (functional and emotional need): there are three components of consumer understanding which are deeply interrelated and equally useful to understanding consumers.

It is thus the market research industry that has to accept the challenge of identifying the insights of the moment so as to be able to allow brands to embrace Post Millennial Marketing, going beyond static profiling and averages:

"*A moment,*" as Rosie Hawkins, Global Director of Client Solutions at Kantar says, "*is an individual experience, defined by the context you are in. In that sense it could include a combination of different things like time, place, what surrounds you, who you are with, what you are doing, your state of mind, the needs and aims and the motivations that move you.*" The relevant moment thus doesn't just have a temporal meaning, but embraces a much wider series of conditions and specific situations in which consumers find themselves, and which could lead them to approach a brand in a way that is completely unusual. "*It is precisely this combination of context factors – moments – that influence the behaviour of consumers, beyond what they think, do and buy.*" Rosie Hawkins continues in the presentation of the new global positioning paper "Unlock the power of the moment" by Kantar TNS[36].

Millennials essentially teach us that we can no longer classify them by lifestyle: it is difficult to state that a Millennial can have a given lifestyle; rather, we ought to recognise that wishes, motivations and needs can be activated and adjusted according to the moment.

It is precisely this capacity to analyse consumers, that goes beyond averages and past behaviour, but rather looks for specific moments of possible connection with a consumer, which allows Post Millennial Marketing to be able to appear at an opportune moment without disturbance: content will appear at the right time, to just the right person, in answer to a real and specific need relating to the context that he or she is experiencing at that moment.

---

[36] www.tnsglobal.com/moments, global positioning paper launched in May 2017.

If today we are unfortunately not able to closely monitor all moments, consumer profiles and needs, before long everything will be connected: objects will be, cars will be, points of sale will be, the things people say during the day will be[37]... and it will thus be a lot easier to work using a Post Millennial Marketing approach. Today we can begin to train ourselves in digital environments, since the use of connected devices (from computers to smartphones, up to connected TV) means that we can track behaviour, profiles and desires in a fairly flexible way, and thus apply Post Millennial Marketing.

---

[37] We should consider the capacity of voice interpretation that is now available on all smartphones or the devices which are being launched at this time, such as Amazon Alexa and Google Home: these are voice-activated virtual assistants to help consumers and to do so store every kind of data.

Surprise with Contents

The world of the Millennials is a great big world, full of new things, opportunities and possibilities of change compared with our old social and economic systems. On the other hand, it has some effects which are not always positive, some of which have great impact on brands: the limited attention span of the consumer, reduced loyalty and a more critical eye, and attention to prices are just some of the greatest difficulties which today's marketing must face.

Another difficulty which comes with implications which are not negligible is the social conformism generated by web environments which tend to put forward past behaviour and a thread of opinions from one's "friends". The social media world has pushed new generations to continually seek out moments of visibility and windows in which to show themselves which end up having a not insignificant impact on the way in which people express themselves and take positions.

What Google gives back as an answer to a search is also based on what we have searched for and clicked on in the past. Facebook and LinkedIn seek to enter into contact with people from our own circle of friends, or at least people who are close to our network. The world of social media is closing us inside a bubble in which opinions are always the same, desires are those of the past, our character is always under control... since we cannot destroy our reputation with a vulgar post, or one that has the wrong tone. There is a lot of research that shows that the polarisation of opinions, including electoral ones, into nuclei of those in favour and against who don't talk to each other much and don't really discuss things: actually brands often end up talking a lot more with their own followers than with prospects.

Post Millennial Marketing sees opportunities in this area: **breaking routines or repetitive mechanisms and leaving – giving us the chance to get away from – the patterns in which we have been imprisoned by through the use of algorithms of our presumed affinity.** The capacity to surprise, in a world that seeks in every way to adapt and pigeon-hole us, will always be more of a competitive advantage and it is the creative challenge that the so-called advertising people are faced with, perhaps even more so than before.

In a certain sense it is a case of making the engineering approach described earlier creative: it will be the content that we send will be in answer to a given moment, a given need, which will make the difference by surprising the consumer.

If you use a search engine or ask your Facebook friends to give you suggestions for a present, or a holiday, what do you get back? Normally, and except in a few odd cases, you get stereotyped answers, because they are based on what the majority of users have done or on what algorithms or friends feel you would like. It is there that a surprise cuts in with all its creative strength, offering the best answer to the moment-profile-need in a way that is completely striking and captivating.

Would you stop and look at this advert?

Imagine that you were in front of a poster in the street, reading a magazine or flicking through your Facebook feed: I think that a lot of you wouldn't hesitate to seek out what they want to say...

Advertising is skipped, it is avoided as soon as possible: a cellphone is the new remote control used for zapping! Content that surprises or makes you marvel is a content that, with pictures, text or video... on any device, will allow the brand to win attention and be memorable.

In the search for the right consumer for the right profile and moment, Marc Pritchard, Global Chief Brand Officer at Procter & Gamble, has admitted feeling that he was caught in a "content crap-trap":

"Trying to do dynamic, real time marketing in this digital era, we have

produced thousands of new television ads a year, with thousands of different agencies and we have made millions of changes in media plans. I imagine that we thought the best way to get noticed in the digital age was to make more adverts and change them exponentially. (...) While the world was becoming more strident and complex, we have simply added noise to noise. The fact that a growing number of consumers choose to skip or block online ads shows that there is a tangible and worrying reaction to this bombardment of brand messages. The people we are talking to are judging with their fingers: they are telling us that a lot of our advertising is unwanted, not interesting, not inspiring and thus ineffective."

Millennials have broken the contract with advertising that allows brands to show messages in exchange for free graphic content (films, events, music, ...), and so new ways are needed that know how to position a company's promotion in a new paradigm of exchange of values.

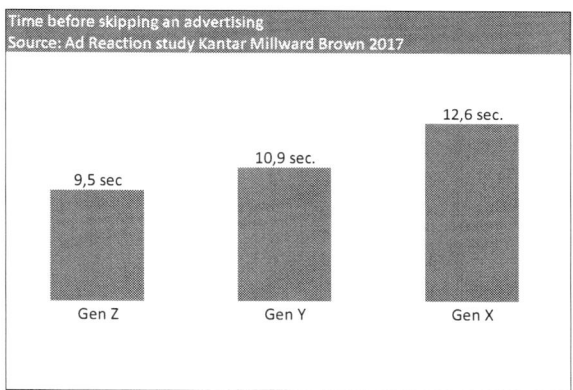

Content Marketing is a discipline that consists of editorial-type, and thus not advertising-type initiatives, which are based on content that is relevant for the life and interests of the reference group, even though it is promoted or sponsored by a brand. The relevance of this kind of initiative for consumers is given by various different factors:

- the **issue** being dealt with, first of all: they touch upon issues which are relevant for the targets at the specific moment in which they are making plans;
- the way it is **executed**: they look more like films or articles, than advertising;
- the **diffusion**: they can be spread on various platforms and devices, without having to limit themselves to thirty seconds of filmed advertising.

In this case too, it doesn't seem a good idea to dwell further on this discipline, since a range of material on Content Marketing is already available and can be freely accessed on the Internet.

Attitude towards brand adv formats
Source: Ad Reaction study Kantar Millward Brown 2017

Diff %pts positive vs negative	Gen Z	Gen Y
Tutorials	46	49
Branded events	43	41
User reviews	42	44
Sponsored events	42	41
Expert reviews	41	42
Social media feeds	37	36
Shopping content	34	34
Brand information	31	37
Native articles	30	31
Social media celebrity content	27	19
Celebrity content	25	19
Magazine advertorials	24	27

But what I do think it is vital to spend some time on is the necessity that this content highlights and/or should be surprising in its narrative and tone of presentation: a piece of content, in a system of attention which is extremely fragmented like the one in today's world, on its own is not enough to attract attention and emerge from millions of other contents which are spread by users or brands, on social media or in real life. Post Millennial Marketing seeks *surprise*: to be able to strike and thus attract attention and be retained, a piece of content has to be creative, according to the most traditional parameters of creativity which are often forgotten today amongst behavioural marketing and programmatic advertising.

"Surprise with content" thus means appearing at moments that are relevant to consumers with contents that can amaze or make people marvel. There are various different techniques used in advertising that now appear to be more relevant than ever, whether we are planning a post on our Facebook page, or are filming an advert to be broadcast on television: from all of them, we choose an effective and simple methodology called Systematic Inventive Thinking (SIT), which has been widely used for over twenty years now. The model offers nine different systems to generate creative and surprising communication elements[38]:

1. **Reduction**: one or more elements of the communication is partially or completely removed so as to emphasise, through its absence, the message or the benefit that is to be communicated
2. **Absurd alternative**: what should be done to achieve a particular goal if you don't want to buy the product is emphasised in an absurd way
3. **Extreme promise**: an extreme promise is created, so as to exaggerate the message and put over how the product can work in extreme situations or how it should be able to do marvellous and unexpected things
4. **Extreme consequence**: the negative effects are shown of an extreme use of the product
5. **Metaphor**: the message is put over through another object that is normally associated with the same concept
6. **Extreme effort**: it tells what people would be prepared to do to own the product or participate in that event

---

[38] See the reworked version by Marco Lombardi in *"Creativity in advertising"* (published by Franco Angeli, 2010)

7. **Inversion**: emphasising the negative effects caused by not following what the brand seeks
8. **Unification**: the initiative or the product is talked about, giving them an additional role compared with the normal and predictable one
9. **Activation**: the public is called upon to participate in an initiative with an active role, communicating the importance of consumer participation to achieve the goal.

We could write thousands of pages if we wanted to spell out the specific marketing, advertising or social media posts which contain an element of surprise. But to do that, you just have to spend a few minutes on a search engine to find blogs, videos or PowerPoints which you can spend some very enjoyable time watching.[39] But what I feel is fundamental is to spend more time on the techniques listed above: originally they were thought up for the generation of creative thought, and then applied to advertising, they are stratagems that can be used in the brand's various different touch points. Think of how to manage, with these techniques, a Facebook page or the first frames of a campaign on pre-roll on YouTube. Choose one or more of these ways to make the content surprising, and you will see that the virality of the initiative is guaranteed. But go further... and from the start consider content and any element of the communication and the offer. The message, the format, the media, the logo are all elements that can be managed in a creative and surprising way. Even the price can be! For Millennials, price is not just the money they should spend in a transaction, but is itself an act of communication from brands: modular packaging, freemium strategies, accessible product lines, co-marketing and portfolio strategies, discounts and promotions, are all techniques that for Post Millennial Marketing express wishes in the relationship with consumers. A high price thus runs the risk of putting over more distance than premium-ness. A surprising and creative pricing system, however, conveys the message that a firm is able to find the right way offer access to its products or services.

---

[39] Link to "TOP Clever Marketing Ideas": https://goo.gl/T49nSn ; Link to "Most creative Advertisement Ideas ever": https://goo.gl/kwOqwN

Facilitate Action

Marketing often spends too much time and money in digital work that is not aimed at sales. The Web2.0 and its collaborative variations in writing brand content (User Generated Content), has led to the conviction that brands in digital environments seen this way are no longer able to communicate in a top-down way, and can no longer do without dialogue with users, that they can't any longer put themselves across as selling things. There is a lot of truth in recognising the special nature of the web as an environment of relationships and not just of communication (advertising or sales), but it is never correct to extremise or put forward dogma.

Going beyond sterile discussions over what is presumably analogue communication and presumably dialogue communication, we feel it is useful in this chapter to look carefully at what can really be obtained – and how – in connected communication environments, however on or offline they are: the thought and relationship system between humans and objects, or even between objects, has by now become like a net, and it will increasingly be like that.

Availability of information and opinions, linked to the ease of connection between them, has a fundamental implication on brand communication. The Internet has taught us that we can no longer distinguish areas by their purpose: there are no longer communication media which have greater affinity to information on a product (which was once mainly the case with the press), or to the promotion of a brand's system of values (which was once mainly the case with television), or to geographical closeness (which was once mainly the case with radio, or billboards), or sales (as was mainly the case with shops).

Some people still put forward these distinctions even within digital communication, identifying creativity and processes aimed at branding (or to the generation of brand awareness or association) or aimed at converting to a lead or purchase, but it is the case of a pure, highly simplistic planning gimmick.

We cannot any longer think in an unrefined and superficial way, by identifying the needs of the brand and thus favouring one media system or another: we have to enter into the moments, to understand profiles and needs, and on that basis, gather as much as possible.

Also, the growth of e-commerce activity and the spread of access channels to be able to make a purchase (from social media to apps), emphasises the option of converting to make a purchase at every moment and chance of contact.

That said, and going beyond potential fragmentation of goals that can be achieved at any moment that can be relevant to consumers, one thing is now clear: the digital world and the proliferation of messages to which consumers are subjected every second, asks us to explain the reasons for communication, the reason why marketing activity, aimed at the individual, has been conceived and implemented. You have to make the job easier for our consumer, and be proactive in the most important moments, with the most engaging creativity, but without ever forgetting to lead them by the hand, to the place (emotional or physical) where we are heading. The digital world is a world of "calls to action", precisely because the state of mind with which the narration is tackled is of an active, interactive, proactive type: consumers interact and do not make use of content and so brands have the chance of putting them in front of a series of paths (links) thanks to which the brand (and the consumer) will be able to reach their goal.

So consumers' actions should be facilitated, through explanations of the next step that means they can reap the benefit (call to action), or by showing the paths – simple and ones with value – through which they can reach to the brand.

Post Millennial Marketing starts from the assumption that users don't have time, and cannot allow themselves to have problems navigating between touch points. They cannot accept confusion or discord; also, the same Post Millennial Marketing assumes that there will be a relationship of transparency and authenticity in communication. These are the reasons why communication should always explain its intentions, and not allow usability interference in reaching its aims and those of the user: each communication element or each marketing activity has to allow users to take a further small step towards the brand, towards continuing using content, towards the site, towards a purchase.

Post Millennial Marketing is thus a standardised type, in the sense that it thinks about the user's consumer journey, even when they have won the Lion advertising awards at Cannes: they are adverts that call for an action, which convoke – as said earlier on the Millennials' approach to accepting challenges and taking part in causes – more or less explicitly, so as to provide the consumer with the idea of being in some way guided and not sat down and abandoned: communication should interpret its own actions as successive steps in approaching a goal, and not as one-shot blows.

So there are two ways in which the "facilitate action" step can be taken:

- either the next step can be **explained** to the user ("call to action"), and they can even be helped with purchase systems identified according to the affinity of the profile with other routes taken toward decision making[40].
- or when there is no need to be so explicit, the communication flow and the marketing plan is projected as if it were a route, a **journey** through which the consumer can be led without friction, breaking inertia step by step. To follow this technique, you have to have followed the previous steps in Post Millennial Marketing, from listening to the message proposition in the "relevant moments": it is precisely the recognition of the moment that generates the opportunity to think in terms of helping the consumer's action.

Both these ways combine badly with marketing which is solely aimed at television advertising, and which doesn't taken any account of the issue of touch points on which consumers will set to work once the thirty seconds are over. With a multi-channel planning approach that is aimed at the consumer journey, individual communication initiatives should include a communication system aimed at helping consumer action, as a bridge between one step and the next, whether this is purchase orientated, orientated around more emotional content, or that of brand branding.

---

[40] Amazon is without doubt the master of this: *"Our mission is to delight our customers by allowing them to serendipitously discover great products"* you can see this in an article published here:
www.fortune.com/2012/07/30/amazons-recommendation-secret/

Enrich Experience

Millennials teach us that the most important factor in relationships with other people and the surrounding world is experience, both that which is experienced and that which has been passed on by word of mouth.

The digital world, as has often been said, is a world that hosts opinions, perceptions, stories of individual experiences; it is not made up of anonymous data and information. Millennials have grown up in this stew of experience and have immediately learned how to make decisions based both on experiences they have been lived and those they have read about: whether expressed through a post, a comment, a like or a rating star... experiences that have been lived are always the rudder which Generation Y uses to steer through the myriad possibilities and opportunities which exist today.

For this reason, young people nowadays don't tolerate companies that don't pay attention to the ways in which they present themselves at moments when they meet them: whether it is a website, an app, a shop or a call centre, the experience generated should be the only thing to which attention is paid. But we are at a time when companies, because of their culture or budget, struggle to ensure high experience levels for their users, and often only pay attention to some touch points and not all of them.

A good customer experience, most of all, means giving clients value. That is why it is so important: companies that have a solid and satisfied client base are those that know how to give consumers a benefit system that isn't restricted to the moment when the product is consumed, or the service used. Experience is nothing other than what we give to the consumer in exchange for the premium price that we charge them. Or put another way, it is what a consumer really pays, in a world in which the benefits from products are massified and often very similar. In other words: a good experience with the brand's various touch points is what competitive capacity depends on. That is especially true for companies that adhere to the Post Millennial Marketing model, since after having called customers to action, they have to be sure that the context in which such an action will take shape is both gratifying for the user and constructive for his or her relationship with the brand.

With the proliferation of touch points created by digital communication platforms, the work of the marketer who aims at excellence from a customer experience point of view has certainly become very complicated: it is no easy matter ensuring the best experience in both the various touch points managed by the company and those not managed by the company (user generated content), so as to give the consumer a coherent, problem-free overall picture. Lining up all the touch points and ensuring that each gives maximum client satisfaction means **implementing flexible and effective management systems, managing information flows in a detailed and timely fashion, and carefully training and monitoring the human resources who are appointed to handle the relationship at each touch point.**

It is also crucial to have a very wide definition of touch points, and one that follows a customer-centric vision: they should be part of the channels to be monitored and on which to take action, not just the various communication channels (on and offline) and the point of sale, but also all the possible "places" where consumers could come into contact with the brand, such as social media, word of mouth, reviews, etc; without forgetting that advertising, including television advertising, or a piece of Corporate Social Responsibility communication, also creates an experience with the consumer and should be treated as such: they are all touch points where experience, and not just the memory, has to be maximised! Customer experience is not actually the assessment of a purely rational experience (which can be measured with KPIs such as telephone reply time, shop opening times, delivery times, etc…): customer experience is what a consumer feels, after assessing rational and emotional aspects, after any interaction with the brand, whether generated by a meeting with a shop assistant or with a piece of communication.

Managing customer experience has thus got to do with the "how" and not just the "what" we supply to our client. The APPLE strategy on this seems fairly important, and can be applied to any other touch point, if you consider:

A: Approach customers with a personalized, warm welcome
P: Probe politely to understand the customer's needs
P: Present a solution for the customer to take home today
L: Listen for and resolve issues or concerns
E: End with a fond farewell and an invitation to return

It is important to have a precise design and feedback system for all our brand's touch points (yes, for all of them!) to then focus the management budget on the most relevant touch points.

The consumer actually goes through various interactions (a Kantar TNS study from 2016 estimates that the consumer goes through at least four different touch points before finishing a purchase; this is a figure that also changes a lot from industry to industry) and it is important to minimise the risk of disconnecting with a careful projection of the touch points on the lines of a customer-centric vision aimed at satisfaction.

Touch Point Customer Experience Check list			
TP ranked on Business Impact	CX design	Feedback	Management
1	x	x	x
2	x	x	x
3	x	x	x
4	x	x	x
5	x	x	x
6	x	x	x
7	x	x	x
8	x	x	x
9	x	x	x
10	x	x	
11	x	x	
12	x	x	
13	x	x	
14	x	x	
15	x	x	
16	x		
17	x		
18	x		
19	x		
20	x		
...	x		

Nevertheless we can recognise that it is always just a few touch points which are responsible for the majority of purchases (20-80 Pareto efficiency is also applicable to this context). Hence, once the key moments in the brand-consumer relationship are known, we can implement accurate and excellent management systems for the main touch points, and they can be chosen according to the budget available and the break-even point between costs and returns.

Connect with brand purpose

The last step in the model is perhaps the most important one, since it is intended to give a long-term sense to all the marketing activity described up to now: touch point fragmentation, linked to the need to have marketing programming (in the IT sense of the word) customised by moment, need and individual, can lead to the brand having expressions of itself that are not coherent between one another, or only briefly so, hunting, amongst other things, for the best experience of the particular event.

It is nevertheless worth remembering that the best-known and most profitable brands in history are ones that mean the same thing to all consumers. Coca-Cola, Lego, Google, or Ford are spokespeople for values to which consumers tends to attribute the same system of meaning in every corner of the world.

What do we do to stay coherent, and to be faithful to one's own DNA so as to make the most of things in the long term, in an environment that is so fragmented and changeable like the current one? Post Millennial Marketing, which was created for – and by – Generation Y, abandons for a moment its focus on brand awareness and on brand image to concentrate on identification, activation and on the communication of its own *brand purpose*: for the consumers of today and tomorrow, it is and will always be more important for a brand to not just satisfy a need of representation, but rather that it should say what the company does for the customer and how it operates in the market.

We can thus say that Post Millennial Marketing introduces some new points of view:

- *from advertising communication to sharing of brand contents*
- *from product/service satisfaction to customer experience*
- *from brand image to brand purpose*

Brand purpose is the reason for the brand, its *raison d'etre*, the reason for its existence for a consumer, a role that it plays for the client. That is the DNA of the brand in Post Millennial Marketing, which explains itself – even through suggestions – by individual marketing activities or with moments of specific communication, aimed at strengthening its leadership on that front. It is important to reconnect all the moments of communication, all the touch points used, all the marketing activity in a higher framework, to give the brand coherence, capitalise on its values, win loyalty and look to the long term.

A good customer relationship, in a reference framework in which the brand takes on the role of a body that issues content and gives value, moves the axis of the relationship from a purely transactional level (I pay a price to consume a product that I like), or of an emotional or aspirational type (I pay a price to present myself in a certain way to others, or for self-representation/self-gratification), to a level of relationship that sees the brand and the consumer moving together towards a shared goal, to obtain a shared value, to shape the same world.

There are different ways in which a brand can emotionally connect the different, daily interactions it experiences with the consumer: taking up a cause, giving service, making available one's know-how, explaining one's values and acting in consequence. From the point of view of execution which can happen in a number of different ways, from the single format of communication, to the coherence between different marketing stimuli (price, quality and product ingredients, the point of sale and communication activity on touch points must be coherent, they must be part of the same brand system), up to Corporate Social Responsibility or the larger institutional campaign.

The most important thing amongst the many activities that have to be deployed to be able to focus marketing on brand purpose, is managing the company's internal human resources: if we were to ask our colleagues what the final goal of the company for which we work is, I am sure that in 99% of the cases we would get answer of the "profit" type. It is not that the answer is actually wrong, all commercial companies must be aimed at making a profit and without that they wouldn't survive, but the company that espouses Post Millennial Marketing must get a different answer. It is like answering that one lives to eat, when in reality one lives to give, to be, to experience. The basis of survival (profit) is one thing; the reason for being is another (purpose).

In relation to this, I will once again quote Marc Pritchard, the Global Chief Brand Officer of Procter & Gamble: *"The brand is like a work of art. You have to explore the angles of the area of the brand to find new ideas and magical creative moments that will help us to keep the brand fresh*

(relevant, author's note). *But wherever you are with this work of art, make sure that you are always seen to be what you are (*unique, author's note*), painting a brilliant masterpiece which is to be looked at and remembered."*
"I love the humanity of Tide. It is a brand for people, made up of people who understand the consumers to whom it is aimed."

Millennial @Work: expectations and realities of Millennials as employees

Lots of people admit it: working with Millennials is really difficult. Especially for bosses. Sometimes they are straining at the leash to grow, to learn, to know, to seek out professional challenges in new areas; and at other times they seem listless, inattentive, inconclusive, unable to follow a mandate and finish a job.

One of the reasons for this paradox lies in their special characteristics, one of which is the ability to adapt. They have grown up adapting to new, emerging worlds, following information, social and cultural flows on the Internet, reacting to trending topics and following any fashion of the moment, right up to the point when they suddenly give it up for the next one. The same capacity, however, can be a boomerang for their growth in a company and for the growth of the company itself: a Millennial that doesn't find their work environment interesting, if they don't feel pricked by stimuli, if they don't see their superiors as authoritative guides to navigate the complexity that they themselves manage to glimpse (and, what is more, with enthusiasm), they will quickly adapt to the anti-S.T.Y.L.E. style.

We have a great responsibility toward them: in just a year we run the risk of ruining them and making them become "1.0". Millennials adapt to the context, they don't challenge it if they don't feel that it is relevant for their survival or gratification. They don't have values to struggle for: the values of the S.T.Y.L.E. that motivate them are rather a grouping of parameters according to which something is valued (specifically a job in this case) as worthy of engagement (and thus worth fighting about) or not.

There are so many work places that don't respect the S.T.Y.L.E. and that is why we often find that Millennials are inattentive, bored and passive. Try asking yourself the following questions, in the marketing team that you head or the company as a whole:

- **S - Sociability**: In your company do you socialise, is networking stimulated, do things happen that you talk about?
- **T - Transparency**: Are you transparent bosses? Do you share strategies

and how things are progressing? Are you open to assessment? Do you co-create or do you inform?
- **Y - Yes, now!**: Are you reactive in relation to what happens, do you interpret current affairs, do you live the present?
- **L - Liberty**: Do you give the option to choose or pre-defined career plans? Do you allow comparison and movement to new units and geographical clusters?
- **E - Experience**: Do you stimulate an entertaining, playful, creative and personal work environment?

When Millennials find a company that respects the S.T.Y.L.E, they see an environment in which they can express themselves and in which they can give value, with enthusiasm and participation. We have a great responsibility to understand them and provide them with the right environment in which to work in line with our own expectations: getting added value from them, critical spirit to the past and inspiration towards the future.

Sometimes, it has to be admitted, we haven't always got all the stimuli to be able to provide Millennials with the right work environment: especially in western countries, we often work in companies which are limited in their ability to redesign organisations, that call for actions which are often connected with significant investments. But that should not curb our desire to bring the best out of the spirit of Generation Y.

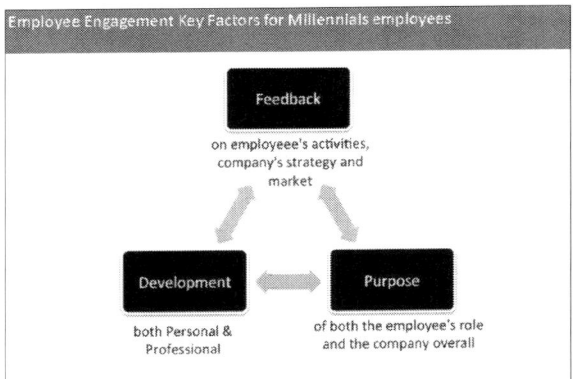

A Post Millennial company, or Post Millennial leaders are actually characterised by recognising, and making their own, three values above everything else:

1. **Feedback**: giving input on work, continually reacting to the actions of Millennials, without judgement but rather to stimulate their continual growth. Think of the obsession that Millennials have for likes and the sharing of content that they post: these tools are essential to them to adjust their camera filters and to manage posting on their Facebook page. In the same way, a feedback on work is an occasion to fine-tune what they do. That is a valid rule if there are lots of employees, but Millennials require constant, daily application in a way that is not necessary for other people.

2. **Purpose**: divide the reason for the task and put it, transparently, into a wider context, providing Millennials with the scope and environment in which they themselves can have an impact. Think of the "convocative" campaigns, as stressed earlier, in which

Millennials take care of a project, philanthropic or otherwise, and make the most of it and promote it in their social media in a personalised way. Within their job, sharing a purpose (of the employee inside the company system and the company mission) explains the expectations and gives value to the relationship, creating the "emotional" sense of the hours spent in the office.

3. **Growth**: this provides the tools and input that Millennials will be able to use to negotiate the complexity of the modern world and what awaits them. They don't ask for predetermined rules, but viewpoints, opinions, new professional tools which can be used so they can handle their professional progression, in a world which is no longer growing linearly. In this case too, think of how they experience Social Media: for Millennials the web is an extraordinary source of opinions, experiences, options and viewpoints.

They are indeed difficult at work, the Millennials: if you let them loose, they don't move, if you order them what to do, they don't reply. But if you orientate them using continual feedback, and by providing them with the purpose of the company and their own particular role, if you give them a clear indication of how you will help them to grow, you will be able to unleash their creativity and the commitment to transformation that a lot of companies today need.

CONCLUSIONS

From a certain time on, everything changed. Young people can't be understood any more, communication media are turning in lower and lower ROI, creativity doesn't get attention, shops are emptying in favour of an app or a website. We have to be honest and harsh: a lot of the old paradigms of brand management and marketing planning don't work any more.

This text has proposed a new framework, Post Millennial Marketing, which starts off from a real and profound understanding of Millennials and Generation Z, to identify the direction of the change and what consumers expect: we have called it "S.T.Y.L.E". It is the set of values which are unique to the new generations which inspire social, economic and individual change in the targets, and which consequently will inspire marketing in the next few years. Embracing S.T.Y.L.E. in brand management, in marketing and communication is a necessity for companies, but which only a few companies manage to fulfill.

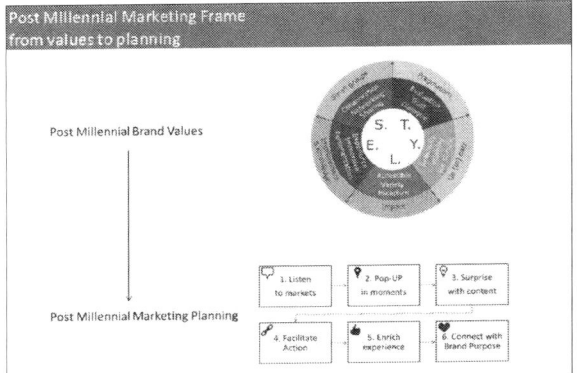

In this context, even marketing planning is set to change significantly,. It can no longer be a simplistic and sequential process of initiatives aimed at the generation of awareness, brand consideration and purchase. Planning nowadays requires greater coordination which can harvest the opportunities generated by the current complexity: the Post Millennial Marketing framework has made the value concepts of S.T.Y.L.E. its own and adapts itself to the lifestyle, consumption, decision and use of media in the post-Millennial world. It is a conceptual framework which can accompany marketing in planning activities, but more than that it is a matter of a stimulus to think and act systematically as our customers do: their S.T.Y.L.E. of consumption should inspire our way of doing marketing, in every discipline, from market research to media planning, to packaging design, to the research of pricing, to distribution choices, to shopper marketing up to involving every other means of communication in the company ecosystem, from PR to CSR work, and right up to internal communication.

It is difficult to draw a conclusion in a text that aims to add some clarity on the extent of the change that is taking place, providing stimuli and tools to deal with a future that is definitely difficult to predict. But, if you have bought this book, you probably don't need to be further convinced as to the urgency of change and the need to escape from Generation X Marketing: if anything you will need to understand how far off your marketing is from the practices of Post Millennial Marketing, for you yourselves or to obtain an incremental budget for the Millennial Transformation.

That is why for the ending I am suggesting a kind of testimony, a moment of passing between the theory of the text and the practice of your daily existence: some of the check lists already shown in the *#Generation2.0* text which will mean that the ideas of this book can be implemented and the application of Post Millennial Marketing can begin.

So go through the questions in the check list below – thinking of how you currently do marketing, or a specific communication activity, a product, or an initiative that you have perhaps even designed for Millennials, and find out if it has the characteristics of the "S.T.Y.L.E". Answer each question with a score of 1 to 10, where 1 means that you don't follow the S.T.Y.L.E. at all, and 10 that you completely follow it. You will thus be able to rate your own initiative.

S.ociability   1   10
the brand, the product, the initiative, …

1. Does it give the chance to meet new people?							
2. Is it something you would talk about with other people?							
3. Does it give the participant a leading role in the group?							
4. Has it (or does it seem as if it has) been created by someone who participates in it?							
5. Can it be shared with others?							
6. Does it say something new or give new prompts?							
7. Can it be changed by the participants themselves?							
8. Can it link up with other initiatives that already exist?							
9. Is there some reason why it should be shared between friends?							
10. Does it allow for customisation and the chance of telling something about oneself?							

T.ransparency   1   10
the brand, the product, the initiative...

1. Is it true to its origins, or to whoever created it?	
2. Is it coherent with other initiatives that have already been carried out?	
3. Does it somehow explain why it was created?	
4. Is it open to assessment?	
5. Does it have a purpose that is implicitly linked to advertising?	
6. Does it talk of real life, of daily existence?	
7. Does it have a language that is immediately understandable?	
8. Does it share the aims of those for whom it was created?	
9. Is it open to failure, or at least to improvement?	
10. Is it close to the way young people are?	

Y.es, now!   1   10
the brand, the product, the initiative, ...

1. Does it relate to anything current?	
2. Can it be done quickly?	
3. Is it progressive, so does it grow over time?	
4. Can you get to it immediately, without going through any intermediate steps?	
5. Is it linked to a phenomenon of the moment that is instant?	
6. Does it stem from the answer to another phenomenon?	
7. Does it suggest "freeze-framing" the moment?	
8. Is it unconnected to an event in the past or the future?	
9. Does it reach full strength at a particular moment, does it have a climax?	
10. Is it unpredictable?	

L.iberty	1						10
the brand, the product, the initiative, …							
1. Does it give room to the participant?							
2. Is it accessible without ties?							
3. Is it applicable in different formats or situations?							
4. Does it have "zero cost" levels that can be joined?							
5. Does it allow the user to actively participate?							
6. Does it allow the user to "do things themselves"?							
7. Does it have a wide range of possibilities?							
8. Does it make what it is about clear with quick previews?							
9. Does it allow different ways of getting the same thing to be evaluated?							
10. Does it allow you to leave and return?							

E.xperience *the brand, the product, the initiative, …*	1						10
1. Is it entertaining in free time?							
2. Can the user get immersed with interactive activities?							
3. Does it offer a personal experience?							
4. Does it stimulate the senses?							
5. Does it reward involvement?							
6. Does it lead people to be more than listeners?							
7. Is it easy to get started?							
8. Does it cut down on frills to concentrate on the heart of the matter?							
9. Does it talk about the meaning and the values behind why it was thought up?							
10. Is it the setting of a story in which a role can be played?							

I hope that the result of the check list is a positive one. In any case, with the end of the book, I can't do anything less than encourage you to find your communication S.T.Y.L.E. as soon as possible and to get marketing.

Wishing you a good start with Post Millennial Marketing!

AFTERWORD

A 52% increase. That is how much the sales of vinyl records have grown in the last year (data from the FIMI, the Italian Music Industry Federation), with a market share that has gone from 3 to 6% in three years. Phono Press, the only and last-surviving vinyl record factory in Italy, has nearly tripled its revenues. In the United Kingdom in 2016 (data from the British Phonographic Industry) the vinyl record market has overtaken that of downloads, reaching 1991 levels. A lot of artists, old and new, have decided to re-issue or release for the first time in vinyl. And the funny thing is that it is not nostalgia driving the boom but young people.

When I talk about Millennials in my programme I always refer to the phenomenon of consumption that I have just described. No other generation, in my opinion, can serve as a bridge both with its predecessor (Baby Boomers and Generation X) and also with the succeeding one (Generation Z or Centennials). They blend together on and offline with extreme awareness and balance, says Federico Capeci in this book: so innovation and tradition. There lies the great potentiality not just of a generation but of an approach (the "Millennial Mindset" to put it as Capeci does) which runs the risk of being under-utilised in all sectors, not just marketing.

Digital entrepreneurs and innovators on one side, and a generation of people without fixed contracts on the other – the Millennials are the most studied generation ever. What is clear is that, as consumers, they are redefining the rules of the market and communication, introducing new drivers in purchase decisions (see the attention paid to sustainability, and also to coherence and the authenticity of products and companies) and new consumption models (the sharing economy and subscription economy above all). And as citizens they have also changed or are changing the rules "from the bottom up", demanding what the digital economy and disintermediation offers from administrations: efficiency, immediate answers, room for participation. And as workers, of course, the Millennials mark a change in paradigm: from their relationships with employers to the physical or virtual spaces where they work, up to operational methods and company organisation. Because, as workers, they still look for that dialogue between peers, which is participatory and collaborative, that they have with the brand as consumers.

Everything lies in working out whether to put them "in attack or on the bench", as the demographer Alessandro Rosina stresses in his reflections on the generation, which reflect the main weak point of Millennials in being that they easily become unmotivated. And a demotivating factor can be a marketing plan, an employer or even a country (see the brain drain phenomenon).

As a journalist and commentator, I feel I have to stress another aspect, however. "Feedback" and "Content", writes Capeci, are two pillars of Post Millennial Marketing. In a situation in which fake news and post-truths are posing questions of the publishing world, journalism, social media and communication as a whole, it will also be for marketing to burst the "filter bubble" approach. These are the bubbles of content, information and opinions through which a part of the Internet (above all our social media walls) tells us about the world. A world that is aligned with and close to our tastes, but which is not the whole world, the real one, outside the door, full of contradictions which can question our convictions. For marketing it will be an act of bravery, because it will be against many of the elements of advertising logic in a strict sense, it will be much less branded and much more unbranded, but it will allow us to dialogue with the stimuli, the requests and the emergencies of our time. This is what the Millennials – and Centennials – are already able to decipher and roll out in their own consumption habits and lifestyle.

Marialuisa Pezzali, Radio 24
Author and presenter of "Essere e Avere" (Being and Having)

BIBLIOGRAPHY

This book is based on research that the author has personally carried out over the past few years. Specifically: from 2003 to 2005 at Coca-Cola Italia, from 2005 to 2008 at OTO Research, from 2008 to 2014 at Duepuntozero DOXA, and since 2015 in Kantar, which is part of the WPP Communication Group. Over these years many people provided inspirations and points of departure for reflection on the writing of this book and how the Post Millennial Marketing model should be set out: teachers, speakers, colleagues and clients have been privileged sources of information and stimuli.mAmongst these, and more than the rest, there has been Elisa Pucci: an extraordinary professional and a special wife.

There are some texts which then have, in different ways, stimulated the thought behind the book, of which below those of greatest and most direct relevance are listed below.

Adams P. (2012). Grouped. How small groups of friends are the key to influence on social web. London, UK: Pearson.
Capeci F. (2014). Generazione 2.0. Chi sono, cosa vogliono, come dialogare con loro. Milan, Italia: Franco Angeli.
Coupland D. (1996). Generazione X. Milan, Italy: Arnoldo Mondadori Editore
Di Falco A., Gibbs D., Corcoran A. (2009). MTV Generation. London, UK: Networks Europe
Fabbris G. P. (2008). Societing. Il marketing nella società moderna. Milan, Italy: Egea.
Feinstein S. (2004). Secrets of the teenage brain. Research-based strategies for reaching and teaching today's adolescents. San Diego, US: The Brain Store.
Giordano A., Cova B., Pallera M. (2012). Marketing non-convenzionale. Milan, Italy: Il Sole 24 ore

Levine R., Locke C., Searls D., Weinberger D. (2001). Cluetrain Manifesto. The end of business as usual. Rome, Italy: Fazi Editore.
Lievrouw L. A., Livingstone S. (2006). Capire i new media. Culture, comunicazione, innovazione tecnologica e istituzioni sociali. Milan, Italy: Hoepli.
Mayer-Schönberger V. e Cukier K (2013). Big Data. Milan, Italy: Garzanti Libri.
Milner H. (2010). The Internet Generation. Tufts University Press.
Palfrey J., Gasser U. (2008). Born digital: Understanding the first generation of digital natives. New York, NY: Basic Books.
Palfrey J., Gasser U. (2009). Nati con la rete. La prima generazione cresciuta su internet. Istruzioni per l'uso. Milan, Italy: Rizzoli.
Rushkoff D. (2014). Presente continuo, Turin, Italy: Codice Edizioni
Shih C. (2011). The Facebook Era. Tapping Online Social Networks to Market, Sell, and Innovate. London, UK: Pearson.
Tapscott D. (2011). Net generation. Milan, Italy: Franco Angeli.
Tapscott D., Williams A.D. (2006). Wikinomics: La collaborazione di massa che sta cambiando il mondo. Milan, Italy: Rizzoli.
Weinberger D. (2002). Arcipelago Web. Milan, Italy: Sperling & Kupfer Editori.
Weinberger D. (2012). La stanza intelligente. Turin, Italy: Codice edizioni.

SITOGRAPHY:

kantar.com
connectedlife.tnsglobal.com
tnsglobal.com/news-centre/intelligence-applied
millwardbrown.com/adreaction
kantarfutures.com
consumerbarometer.com

Printed in Great Britain
by Amazon